THE PRACTICAL MONEY MANAGER

The Practical Money Manager

A GUIDE AND WORKBOOK ON HOW TO HANDLE YOUR MONEY PROFITABLY IN TODAY'S ECONOMY

Robert H. Persons, Jr.

Charles Scribner's Sons / NEW YORK

Library of Congress Cataloging in Publication Data
Persons, Robert H 1922–
The practical money manager.
1. Finance, Personal. 2. Saving and investment.
I. Title.
HG179.P43 332'.024 74-12218
ISBN 0-684-13978-2

This book published simultaneously in the
United States of America and in Canada—
Copyright under the Berne Convention

1 3 5 7 9 11 13 15 17 19 c/c 20 18 16 14 12 10 8 6 4 2

Printed in the United States of America

Contents

Part III

HOW TO BEGIN MAKING EXTRA MONEY— LOW-RISK INVESTMENTS

Part IV

HOW TO INSURE YOUR "EDGE"—REDUCING THE RISKS WHILE INCREASING THE RETURNS

Part V

BACKING UP YOUR INVESTMENTS

Introduction

The Aim—A New Financial Plan to Make You Self-Reliant and Flexible in the 1970's

The over-riding objective of this book is quite simple: to develop sensible rules for guiding family financial planning in today's economy, when the earning, spending, and investing of family funds will most likely take place in an atmosphere that will include whiffs and perhaps more of inflation, deflation, and devaluation. All of these features of our economy look as if they will be with us for the immediately foreseeable future.

There is little as yet, despite Phase I, Phase II, Phase III, and Phase IV that would suggest that inflation is something that can safely be forgotten in the U.S. economy. The objectives of these economic plans did not include zero inflation rates and implementation of the pay and price guidelines continued to let considerable inflationary pressure loose in the economy. Nor are there any plausible "game plans" in sight that promise to halt inflation in its tracks. So the prudent family should be prepared for at least a little inflation.

At the same time, our inability to compete at home and abroad in many important product lines suggests that at least some areas of our economy are in for a rather painful adjustment period in the 1970's, which will tend to deflate values in a number of industries. Even without the pressure of foreign competition, we as a nation are being forced into an agonizing reappraisal of many of our priorities.

Some of the things we are currently doing are likely to be sharply curtailed before the 1970's are over while others may be greatly expanded.

Moreover, in some instances, these changes are not likely to be gentle or gradual, but may come with the suddenness of a decree from Washington when enough evidence has accumulated that certain practices are harmful or non-beneficial. This is yet another reason to expect some sharp deflationary tendencies to be at work throughout most of the 1970's.

Although the decision has been made to devalue the dollar in terms of gold by requiring $42.22 rather than $38.05 to buy an ounce of gold, there are many problems still remaining on international money markets and in international trade that have not been solved by devaluation. Negotiations will continue in 1974 and beyond to hammer out workable solutions to many of these as yet unresolved questions. But, if the current "solution" to the international exchange problem continues to hold in the 1970's, then formal "devaluations" will be a thing of the past. However, the international purchasing power of the U.S. dollar will be subject to almost continuous "re-evaluation" on the world money exchanges.

Furthermore, current estimates of the dollar liability claims still in the hands of foreigners put them at around $100-billion, or about twice the $50-billion estimated in the summer of 1971, with some $20-billion of this higher $100-billion being considered "hot money"—that is, highly mobile funds ready to move on short notice. Until now, the expected flood of dollars back home has failed to materialize. As a result, the dollar will remain defensive on international money exchanges until either these "hot" dollars come home or money speculators are content with dollar holdings.

All of this leaves at least one aspect of the dollar crisis unchanged—it is only the forebearance of the dollar creditors that prevents a run on Treasury gold. Any loss of confidence, or even some pique at the negotiating table about the terms of international trade on the part of one (or more) European holder of dollar claims, could touch off another monetary crisis, driving down the dollar below acceptable limits. In addition, there will be the increasing flood of dollars that the U.S. must pay to foreign producers of oil as the price per barrel settles in at much higher levels than formerly. So don't rule out further devaluation in the 1970's.

With analysis unable to reject completely the possibility of further inflation, or selective deflation, or even another devaluation of the dollar, the problems of the family financial planner will be increased in the 1970's, adding greatly to the number that usually vex him even in more settled times.

Two rules should be given high priority for the 1970's:

(1) *Stay flexible.* Never commit yourself so deeply that it will be ruinous to head for the exits.

(2) *Learn to be a self-reliant investor.* Do not put your money into anything you do not understand. You may have to get out in a hurry, and if you do not fully understand what you have been doing, you may not have time to ask your expert adviser, even assuming he knows both sides of the trade on which he has assured you.

It is with this background that we will take a hard, detailed, and thorough look at how to manage our money intelligently and where to put it most profitably.

The key to financial flexibility is knowing where to find cash. And the cash customer can usually get what he wants on financial markets.

In Part I, we will take a close look at the procedures for constructing a workable family budget, always watching for additional sources of cash that can be used to keep you both solvent and self-reliant in the 1970's.

Part I

GETTING MORE OUT OF WHAT YOU HAVE NOW

CHAPTER 1

Totaling Up Your Actual Worth—And the Amount You Have to Work With

Few of us realize how much money passes through our hands in an ordinary working lifetime. Even assuming a fairly late start of settling down to a first real job at age 25, most of us will spend some 40 years at one job or another until retirement at age 65. Some of us start earlier and others hold down jobs after 65; but even assuming the more conservative 40-year period, lifetime earnings, when added up, are impressive:

AVERAGE ANNUAL EARNINGS	TOTAL LIFETIME INCOME (ASSUMING 40 YEARS ON THE JOB)
$ 8,000	$ 320,000
10,000	400,000
12,500	500,000
15,000	600,000
17,500	700,000
20,000	800,000
22,500	900,000
25,000	1,000,000

Now, a large proportion of us will never reach the higher rungs of the average annual earnings column. At present, only about 30% of all U.S. families can expect to average above $10,000 a year in their working lifetimes. It is now projected that sometime in the 1970's over 50% of all U.S. families will be earning incomes of $10,000 or more. But before you become too enthusiastic, remember that there is likely to be some inflation built into these projected higher family earnings figures. These are money wages, not real wages.

Of course, these totals represent earned income on a job. Most of us also have set aside at least some modest rainy day savings. How do such savings add to our worth?

In the income ranges from $8,000 to $25,000, those families that have been both lucky and prudent over the years may have been able to accumulate at least three months of earnings, or one-fourth of their average annual earnings, and have them available as savings. Some of these savings will be in banks, some may be in cash, and some may even be in the form of a valued possession that can be sold or pawned. But let us assume for convenience that all of these rainy day savings are held in a savings account that earns 5% annually compounded. Granting this, it is evident that families in these income ranges with successful savings plans will have at least some additional funds beyond their regular job earnings.

AVERAGE ANNUAL EARNINGS	SAVINGS (¼ OF ANNUAL EARNINGS)	ANNUAL INTEREST (5%, ASSUMING IT IS NOT COMPOUNDED)	TOTAL INTEREST (COMPOUNDED FOR 40 YRS. AT 5%)
$ 8,000	$2,000	$100	$12,080
10,000	2,500	125	15,100
12,500	3,125	156	17,875
15,000	3,750	188	22,650
17,500	4,375	219	26,425
20,000	5,000	250	30,200
22,500	5,625	281	25,975
25,000	6,250	312	37,750

If we live charmed lives, we may never have to dip into these rainy day savings and be able to walk away with moderately attractive sums at the end of our working lives—for instance, with $17,600 on $10,000 average annual earnings (the original savings of $2,500 *plus* the $15,100 in interest compounded for 40 years), or with $35,200 on $20,000 yearly earnings (the original $5,000 plus the $30,200 in interest). Even if we are relatively unlucky, we will have between $100 and $300 each year to supplement our wages. This possibility is all the more appealing in that it does not result from any wild, speculative scheme, but simply being mildly prudent in handling our family financial affairs.

There is yet another asset that bulks large in most families' financial picture, and that is a house. Over 60% of U.S. families are home-owners, and the percentage is probably higher in the over $8,000 annual income ranges. (If you are not a home-owner, console yourself with the fact that you probably have the down payment invested and are earning a tidy rate of return—see Chapter 3. Assuming that you are a home-owner, at retirement you presumably will have paid off the mortgage and thus will have an asset that can be turned into cash. Even before retirement, you will have some equity in your home that can be realized either by selling your home, or refinancing your mortgage (for some guidelines here, see Chapter 3).

Let's assume that you are living in a house you can afford at your annual income. Your house should be worth 2 to 2½ times your annual income. Using the conventional rule-of-thumb, let us use the figure of 2½ times your average annual income. While this may give an estimated value for your home higher than your original purchase price (hopefully, you were able to buy it at a price closer to 2 times your average annual earnings) it does give us a conservative estimate of possible appreciation that may become available when you finally decide to sell. (Remember, we are talking about income *before* taxes.)

AVERAGE ANNUAL EARNINGS	ESTIMATED VALUE OF HOME (ASSUMING 2½ TIMES INCOME)
$ 8,000	$20,000
10,000	25,000
12,500	31,250
15,000	37,500
17,500	43,750
20,000	50,000
22,500	56,250
25,000	62,500

Finally, you most likely have other assets—such as an automobile, china and silverware, musical instruments, possibly a boat—that can be sold, or pawned in an emergency. You probably have some life insurance, but since we are interested here in how much cash you will have available to support your financial plans—your total capacity for acquiring financial assets—

you should count only the cash value, not the face value (see Chapter 4).

In sum, for most families, without inheritances, their total capacity for acquiring financial assets is the sum of their lifetime earnings, their rainy day savings, the equity they have in their home, plus a miscellany of other possessions with modest current value. Still, the net worth of most families—what they could raise in a pinch—is greater than many realize.

For instance, take individuals earning an annual average of $12,500. In our examples, they will have $3,125 in rainy day savings that can be used in an emergency; they probably have at least the normal 25% down payment as equity in a $31,250 home—or about $7,800 that can be made liquid by the sale of the home or through secured borrowings. In addition, they may be able to raise as much as $1,000 quite easily from the sale of other assets, or by borrowing against the cash value of their permanent life insurance. This adds up to about $12,000—or an amount about equal to their annual income of $12,500.

Let's take this example further.

Beyond the $12,000, these individuals have their current average $12,500 annual income and the prospects of earning $500,000 over their working lifetimes. These figures can also be used to affect one's net worth. Within limits, by resorting to saving and borrowing, families can rearrange the timing of their lifetime incomes. By saving out of current income, they can supplement their future earnings (or retirement income). By borrowing, they can spend some of their future income before it is earned.

How much of this future income will lenders let you bring into the present? Much depends on how you propose to spend the retimed income. For example, 75% of the value of a home is commonly available through mortgages. For our individuals earning $12,500 a year, this means that they can get around $23,500 of their expected $500,000 lifetime earnings from mortgage lenders to pay for a $31,500 home in the present. In an extreme emergency, they might be able to make most of the downpayment tied up in the house available through a second mortgage, if they are willing and able to pay the high interest rates on these types of mortgages.

Banks will lend preferred customers as much as $5,000 on signature loans. But if our individuals earning $12,500 are not in this select company at the bank, they will probably be able to walk away with only about 10% of their take-home (after-tax) yearly income, or about $1,000, depending on their deductions.

Another way to get a fix on your borrowing capacity is to look at the limits most lenders place on installment loans. Many lenders feel that excluding mortgage payments, total payments on all types of one, two, and three year loans should not exceed 15 to 20% of monthly take-home pay. This would give our individuals earning $12,500 the capacity to borrow about $2,500 on bank installment and signature loans over a 12-month period.

If our individuals put this $2,500 in short-term borrowing capacity together with the $23,500 in mortgage money, it is evident that those earning $12,500 can bring between $25,000 and $26,000 of their $500,000 lifetime earnings into the present, or about 5%. This sum is about twice their present before-tax income of $12,500. If they further put this together with the $12,000 that they could raise by wiping out their rainy day savings, liquefying the equity in their homes through a second mortgage or refinancing, and taking the market value of other assets, then it is apparent that the average family is capable of raising a sum equal to at least *three times* their present pre-tax incomes by turning assets into cash and borrowing.

Whether any family should in fact embark on such a program is another matter. Here, we are concerned only with the *limits* of the capacity to rearrange lifetime income and change the mix of assets held—and three times your average expected annual money income, before taxes, seems to give a fairly good approximation of these limits.

Of course, like any rule-of-thumb, this 3-for-1 rule, for relating your cash-borrowing capacity to your earnings, should be applied with caution. Any decisions making use of it should be made only after all of the special features of your own financial affairs have been examined in great detail. For this purpose, the following worksheets have been provided to help you estimate your own lifetime earnings capacity and your own personal limits for raising cash and borrowing.

You might start by defining what you are worth now:

A FINANCIAL PROFILE WORKSHEET

(1) WHAT I OWN

Cash (in your pocket and in the bank)	$ ____ __
Money owed me (if you think they will pay)	$ ____ __
Personal property (furniture, etc. Put down only what you think it could bring if offered for sale now)	$ ____ __
Automobile (what the market would give you)	$ ____ __
Investments (stocks, bonds, etc.—use market value not what you paid)	$ ____ __

Life insurance (cash value *only*) $_____ __
Real estate (home and other—again use what you think the market would give you) $_____ __
Other assets (be realistic) $_____ __

Total $_____ __

(2) WHAT I OWE

Money owed (I.O.U.'s and personal loans) $_____ __
Installment contracts (put down the *total* payments still due on your car, etc.) $_____ __
Accounts owed stores, etc. (only make an entry here if you typically let your current bills run over several months) $_____ __
Mortgages on home and other property (put down the total still outstanding—you just credited yourself with current market values under WHAT I OWN above) $_____ __
Other debts $_____ __

Total $_____ __

(3) WHAT I AM WORTH

Last line from WHAT I OWN $_____ __
Last line from WHAT I OWE,
deduct (–) $_____ __

Net Worth Now $_____ __

(4) WHAT I AM EARNING NOW (monthly)

Monthly salary and wages, current $_____ __
Interest and/or dividends ($1/12$ of annual) $_____ __
Other income ($1/12$ of annual) $_____ __

(5) WHAT I PLAN TO SPEND EACH MONTH

Rent (or if you own your home, INTEREST ONLY in monthly mortgage payments plus property taxes at $1/12$ of annual) $_____ __
Food (including lunches and eating out) $_____ __
Heat—fuel ($1/12$ of annual) $_____ __
Utilities (lights, gas, water) $_____ __
Telephone $_____ __
Clothing ($1/12$ of annual outlays) $_____ __

Transportation (all auto expenses, including $\frac{1}{12}$ auto insurance, plus carfare) $ ____ __

Health ($\frac{1}{12}$ of annual doctor bills and medical insurance) $ ____ __

Education ($\frac{1}{12}$ of annual cost) $ ____ __

Taxes—personal income taxes ($\frac{1}{12}$ of annual) $ ____ __

Interest (*only* on personal and installment loans—monthly payments *minus* repayment of principal $ ____ __

Life insurance ($\frac{1}{12}$ of annual premium *minus* any increase in cash surrender value) $ ____ __

Other insurance ($\frac{1}{12}$ of annual premium on homeowners policy—auto insurance should be under transportation, medical insurance under health) $ ____ __

Vacation and travel ($\frac{1}{12}$ of annual cost) $ ____ __

Recreation and entertainment $ ____ __

Other regular monthly spending $ ____ __

Total Monthly Spending $ ____ __

(6) WHAT I PLAN TO SAVE EACH MONTH

Savings in the bank, bonds, etc. $ ____ __

Payment of principal (equity build-up) in your monthly mortgage payments (put the rest of your monthly mortgage payment under rent in WHAT I PLAN TO SPEND above) $ ____ __

Repayment of the principal on personal and installment loans—you are building the equity in a real asset—put the interest under WHAT I PLAN TO SPEND EACH MONTH above) $ ____ __

Contributions to retirement plans (including Social Security payments) $ ____ __

Life insurance ($\frac{1}{12}$ of the annual increase in the cash surrender value—you counted the *protection* share of your premium in WHAT I PLAN TO SPEND EACH MONTH, above) $ ____ __

Other savings $ ____ __

Total Monthly Savings $ ____ __

(7) SUMMARY OF MY CURRENT FINANCIAL PLAN

Last line from WHAT I AM EARNING NOW $ ____ __

deduct (–)

Last line from WHAT I PLAN TO SPEND EACH MONTH $ ____ __

MONTHLY SAVING (difference between monthly earnings and spending) $____ __

NOW, *deduct* 1/12 estimated annual depreciation on assets owned (car, house, etc.—if you have paid for a vacation on the installment plan, deduct the full principal amount borrowed) $____ __

Net Monthly Savings $____ __

Now go back and compare Net Monthly Savings with the last line of WHAT I PLAN TO SAVE EACH MONTH. *If there is a wide difference between these two numbers, then either you are kidding yourself, or you made an error in arithmetic.* If there is a difference, reconcile them and come up with a new number—Adjusted Net Monthly Savings.

Take Net Worth Now (from WHAT I AM WORTH) $____ __

add (+)

ADJUSTED NET MONTHLY SAVINGS *times* 12 (annual savings) $____ __

What I Plan to Be Worth at the End of the Year $____ __

If WHAT I PLAN TO BE WORTH AT THE END OF THE YEAR is below (which could happen if your monthly spending is greater than your monthly saving), or only a fraction above WHAT I AM WORTH NOW, then you need to do some serious family financial planning. You might start by coming up with some estimation of your earnings from all sources in the years remaining in your working lifetime. This will give you some idea of your capacity to acquire financial assets in the future to make a better showing in NET WORTH NOW at the end of future years.

WHAT I EXPECT TO EARN, IN THE FUTURE

Average estimated annual salary and wages $____ __

Average annual interest and dividends anticipated $____ __

Average annual income from other sources $____ __

Average Expected Annual Income $____ __

deduct (–)

Last line from WHAT I PLAN TO SPEND EACH MONTH, above, *times* 12 (this assumes that your monthly spending patterns will be roughly the same in the future. If this gives too low an estimate, add something for your hoped for rise in living levels) $____ __

Funds Available to Make Net Worth Grow $____ __

If the Funds Available To Make Net Worth Grow calculated above are extremely low, zero, or negative even after allowing for some extra lift in your future earnings power, then clearly you have real financial planning problems. But, even if the funds available for financing future growth—while positive and reasonably creditable—are still well below your aspirations, you may want to do something about it. Either way, you have only two ways to get the number positive and larger.

(1) Go back and examine WHAT I PLAN TO SPEND EACH MONTH and find ways to *spend less,* or . . .
(2) Find ways to make the low, or inadequate, growth funds available to your family *earn more.*

Examining these two possibilities is what the rest of the book is about. For the rest of Part I, we will look at ways you can find to spend less. Then, in Part II, we will discuss some financial housekeeping details—such as where to put your money until you need it, how and when to borrow, and taxes. After that, in Parts III, IV, and V, we will tackle the problem of how to earn more with funds left over after meeting all current expenses and obligations.

CHAPTER 2

Getting the Most from Your Consumer Dollar— I. Necessities and Luxuries

Although what the economic statistician calls consumer non-durable goods and services account for less than half of the budget of the average U.S. consumer (the durable goods that account for over 50 per cent of total household spending are shelter, transportation, and insurance protection—these are discussed in the next two chapters), this kind of spending tends in reality to be the most stable, year in and year out. The main reason for this is that most non-durable goods and services are things that get used up and have to be purchased again.

Not all, to be sure. Some spending here represents pure whim and impulse—rhinestone dog collars, bamboo backscratchers, plastic busts of Joe Namath, etc. But the "necessities" are found here—food (20–25% of the average family's budget); clothing (it hovers around 10% of the family budget); and at least until quite recently, haircuts.

Bread is a prime example of a "pure" non-durable good—it is used up quickly, it has to be replenished, and it is perishable. In recent years, more and more "non-durables" are living up to their name. Shoes are an example. We used to expect them to last. But partly as a result of shoddier quality shoes on the market and the high cost (and disappearance) of repairmen, fewer shoes get resoled today. This is also true of a number of things like small appliances, watches, and radios—it is almost as cheap to replace them with new purchases as to have them repaired, assuming you can find someone to repair them. And the mounting piles of solid waste garbage seem to bear out that we are living in a society that increasingly regards physical goods as disposable.

This has not made it any easier for the average consumer who would like to get value for his consumer dollar spent. Increasingly, he is lost in a welter of plastics, "wonder" fabrics, and new, improved soaps and detergents. Nor has the sharp inflation in consumer prices helped, since price has become a less reliable guide than ever to the quality of the merchandise being bought. As a result, some consumers have turned to the reports of organizations that test consumer products, like Consumer Union of Mount Vernon, New York, to help them determine the quality of a bewildering array of products. If you are sincerely interested in quality and getting what you pay for, you might consult *Consumer Reports Magazine* for informed, expert guidance.

But in a great many areas, the average household shopper—most frequently the housewife—finds herself very much on her own. If she has the time and the energy, she can try to be her own comparison shopper. If she is a rapid calculator or a careful reader of the recently mandated "truth in packaging" labels, she can tell whether a 1 lb. 2-oz. package of a product at 36¢ is a better buy than a 19-oz. package of the same product at 40¢.

What general guidelines are useful to follow? With the high cost of repairs, it probably pays to stay clear of the second-hand markets for anything with moving parts that may need replacing; but there is nothing wrong with second-hand furniture, if the table and chairs can stand on their legs without wobbling. Many communities now have firms that will rent you almost anything, from a banquet service for a hundred to a power saw. For seldom-used items, it is worth investigating.

More specifically, you might try "seasonal" buying, especially in such things as fresh fruits and vegetables. Usually when the crops are harvested, the flow to market peaks and helps drive down their prices, although in recent years rising costs of packaging, transportation, and distribution have tended to keep seasonal fruits and vegetables from dipping in price as noticeably as they once did. Below is a list of fruits and vegetables, showing the percentages of the total annual crop shipped in each month. (Only fruits or vegetables with 20% or more of their annual total shipped in a given month are listed.) An asterisk indicates the peak percentages.

January

Tangerines (21%)

February

None (use cans—frozen vegetables usually more expensive)

March

Asparagus (20%)

April

Asparagus (34%)*
Rhubarb (20%)

May

Asparagus (27%)
Rhubarb (27%)*
Strawberries (27%)*

June

Apricots (55%)*
Blueberries (29%)
Cantaloupes (21%)
Cherries (44%)*
Mangoes (31%)*
Peaches (24%)
Strawberries (27%)
Watermelons (29%)

July

Apricots (37%)
Blueberries (38%)*
Cantaloupes (22%)
Cherries (43%)
Mangoes (24%)
Nectarines (33%)
Plums-prunes (30%)
Watermelons (30%)*

August

Blueberries (26%)
Cantaloupes (25%)*
Nectarines (38%)*
Peaches (27%)
Plums-prunes (31%)*

September

None

October

Persimmons (27%)
Pomegranates (33%)
Pumpkins (79%)*

November

Cranberries (52%)*
Persimmons (42%)*
Pomegranates (33%)
Tangelos (40%)*
Tangerines (22%)

December

Cranberries (21%)
Persimmons (23%)
Tangelos (37%)
Tangerines (45%)*

Another kind of seasonality is the man-made kind of sales and clearances that can give you better buying opportunities. The schedules for regular seasonal sales are given below:

Item	*Best Time to Buy It*
Air Conditioners	July
Appliances and Housewares	January
Automobiles	August, December

Barbecue Sets	August
Boys' Suits	late April (check Easter)
Camping Equipment	August
Children's Clothing	*late* September
China, Glass & Silverware	February, October
Fabrics	June
Fishing Equipment	October
Furniture	January, June
Furniture, summer	August
Furs	August
Garden Supplies	July
Ice Skates	March
Lawn Mowers	August
Lawn Sprinklers	August
Linen ("White Sales")	January, May, August
Lingerie	January
Mattresses & Bedding	February
Men's Shirts	February, November
Men's Summer Suits	July
Men's Suits & Coats	January, late April (check Easter), November
Rugs & Carpets	May, September
Skis	March
Spring Clothing	March
Summer Clothing	June
Summer Sporting Equipment	July
Winter Clothing	January
Women's Dresses	late April (check Easter), November
Women's Hats	late April (check Easter)

Women's Summer Sportswear	May
Women's Winter Coats	November
Yard Tools	August

Let's look at some general purchase areas now.

Food. If you are interested in finding some place to cut back in your spending on non-durables, food, accounting for 20–25% of the average family's budget, is a good place to look. You may have a defeatist attitude about your ability to cut corners here, but remember that most gourmets consider the French and the Chinese cuisines the two outstanding ones in the world, and the secret of both is found more in art and seasoning than in expensive ingredients. In fact, some say that the art of French cooking emerged from the efforts of the frugal French housewives to find ways to use cheaper cuts of meat. So get yourself a good cookbook and a generous spice rack and cut your food bills.

Consumer counselors say that most families can save between $200 to $400 a year on food alone by introducing careful shopping practices. Here are some of the things these expert shoppers advise:

(1) A shopping list that you stick to is essential—*avoid impulse buying.*
(2) Introduce variety through carefully planned menus rather than through a high-priced luxury food bought on the spur of the moment.
(3) Avoid "convenience" packaged foods. There is little value here—"lightly" breaded shrimp typically contains only about 65% shrimp, and frozen chicken dinners are only about 18% chicken. Also, the grocer's profit margin is higher on frozen food—27.8%, on average, for frozen foods as compared with only 21.7% for meat.
(4) Keep your mind only on food while you are in the grocery store. Stay away from the aisles whose shelves are stocked with cosmetics, housewares and apparel. Buy these things elsewhere. Your grocer makes more money on these items than he does on the meat and food—that's why he has devoted more shelf space to them in recent years. But you will do better in other stores.

Clothing. American families have been spending less on clothing in recent years, so economies you are able to introduce here are less likely to be noticed by your neighbors than they would have been several years ago. Families typically spend between 10–12% of their annual budgets on clothing, including laundry and cleaning bills (the increased use of permanent-press and "bulk" cleaning having helped to cut the total spending on clothing). If you shop for clothing on impulse or only when it is worn out, you are likely to spend as much as one-third more than if you plan ahead and shop the sales. Locate the regular season sales on clothing in the table earlier in this chapter, inventory your wardrobe, and save on your clothing outlays.

Medical expenses. Medical expenses have been mounting and taking a bigger slice out of many family budgets in recent years—6–8% being average. Most families share the risk and expenses through medical insurance, with the cheapest coverage available through group plans where you work (see the next chapter for a discussion of private plans). So most people are already pretty well limited in their ability to find places to cut spending for medical care. Hence, until we have a national health plan, the chief way to save money here is to stay healthy. (And don't forget your dentist; get some dental floss.)

All of the rest. Once you have paid for food, clothing, and doctor bills and remember that housing, transportation, and insurance take slightly over 50% of most family budgets, you can see that most families have very little room left to maneuver—somewhere between 10–15% of the total budget having to be spread among such things as appliances, TV, furniture, entertainment, recreation, vacations, education, tobacco, and alcoholic beverages. What you can do here depends on your talents and your tastes—family camping is cheaper than resorts; home-canning is one way to beat the poisons in the additives present in many commercial products; some people mix their own organic cosmetics; a sewing machine and a little patience can work wonders. In general, in all walks of life today there is probably more prestige in what you can do as opposed to what you can *buy.* You might give it a try and have more dollars to add to your family's nestegg.

What about the general climate in which you will be spending your dollars on consumer non-durables in the 1970's: is there any better way to defend yourself against inflation, deflation, and devaluation?

Normally, the only way to beat inflation on things you use every day is to buy ahead of the price rises. But there are problems. You can't stockpile services like medical care. For many clothing items, there's the question of style; and growing children seem to have longer arms and bigger feet every time you look. Food is perishable or bulky and hard to store. So buying ahead has limited usefulness for things that need constant replenishing. The only sensible approach in this area is to shop wisely, bank or invest your savings, and let the interest help cushion the price rises when you re-buy.

Deflation, if it is to come, poses few buying problems, rather the opposite.

In a deflationary situation, prices are lowered and some businesses no longer able to compete at home or abroad are forced to write-down their investments in obsolete machines and to try to strike out in new directions. The only difficulty, of course, is if the machines *you* have been tending happen to be those that become obsolete. But if you and/or your wife can keep a paycheck coming in, shopping for things like food and clothing can be pleasant in a time of weakening prices. Just don't go on a wild buying spree—this is the time, when real savings are possible, to really make some headway in adding to your family's net worth. Remember, if businesses are liquidating their past mistakes, your paycheck can go into the melting pot along with the scrap metal. But if you select some of the defensive ways to protect your savings and earn safe returns—even when business liquidations are everyday occurrences—you will not only survive a deflation but will be in a position to profit from the opportunities presented in this period. (Parts II and III review the ways to protect yourself.) The worst time to have money is when everybody has a lot; the best time to have money is when no one else has any.

Further devaluation—additional increases in the number of dollars it takes to buy an ounce of gold or acquire a unit of a foreign currency—cannot be ruled out for the near future. In fact, with the newly instituted system of flexible international exchange rates, fluctuations in the international purchasing power of the dollar may become monthly, weekly, or even daily events. This is especially true since foreigners still have dollar claims equal to several times as much gold as the U.S. Treasury has on hand in its vaults.

What effect on prices will devaluation have? Devaluation increases the cost of items produced abroad. When it comes to buying things like food, clothing, and other things that have to be re-stocked periodically, the impact of any possible future devaluations will be small. This is largely because 80–90% of the small consumer items most families buy are still made, or at least assembled, in the U.S. despite the inroads by foreign manufacturers in recent years. And other items, like foreign oil or natural gas, whose price would be increased by devaluation, are difficult for the average family to stockpile. But there are some things that it might pay to stockpile when you feel another round of "devaluation" or downward "floating" dollars is due. For example, suppose you like French wine. If you stock up before the dollar weakens further, it will cost you less.* In general, it might pay for you to review your shopping list of foreign wares and

* In the case of wine, there is another good reason to stockpile—wines of good vintage years cost less in the first year or so after they become available, with superior years soaring in price in later years, as the fixed supply is exhausted.

initiate a systematic accumulation program to acquire these things ahead of further devaluations of the U.S. dollar. If you wait until another international monetary crisis is on the front pages, many of these things will already be selling at a premium, or simply be unavailable.

In the next chapter, we will look for money-saving ideas in your expenditures for shelter and transportation.

CHAPTER 3

Getting the Most from Your Consumer Dollar— II. Housing and Transportation

Billy Rose once gave some good investment advice: "Don't buy anything you have to paint or feed." While this advice is sound enough, it is often difficult to put into practice. For most families, this would rule out owning a home; and the family automobile usually has a voracious appetite.

But let's not jump to hasty conclusions. After all, you can rent a house; and you can lease a car, or take the bus (or at least you can take the bus in the few communities where public transportation still exists). While we cannot put a price tag on the somewhat mixed pleasures that come from owning your own home or car, we can at least add up what it costs to paint and feed these possessions. Let's start with shelter, the largest single item in most families' budgets—generally 25–30% of it.

We have already taken a look at the prices of houses that might be owned by families at various income levels (see Chapter 1). The principle we used was that a family was likely to have a house whose value is equal to two and a half times the annual income. Thus, a family whose income is expected to average $10,000 over time might consider a $25,000 home. With this example in mind, let us work out the arithmetic of owning vs. renting.

To keep the arithmetic simple, let us assume that this family can find a suitable rental house or apartment for a $250 monthly rental. Again for the sake of simplicity, let us assume that the utility bills will be roughly the same in the house as in the apartment, or rented house. Next, suppose that a 30-year mortgage is available and that monthly payments on the house total about $300 (mortgage payments—both interest and principal, upkeep, property taxes, and home insurance). Now we are in a position to compare the costs of owning and renting.

FINANCIAL PICTURE OF OWNING A HOUSE FOR 30 YEARS

Buys House at Cost of	$ 25,000
Down Payment	4,500
Leaving for financing	$ 20,500
Monthly Out-of-Pocket Expenses (including monthly payments on 30-year mortgage, upkeep, property taxes and house insurance)	300
Annual Out-of-Pocket Expenses ($300 times 12)	3,600
30-Year Out-of-Pocket Expenses ($3,600 times 30)	108,000
Total Outlay ($4,500 down payment + $108,000)	112,500
Minus Estimated Tax Deductions Available to Homeowners over 30 years	10,500
Total Expenses, after Tax Adjustment	$102,000
Deduct Approximate Market Value of 30-Year-Old House (assuming "normal" rate of inflation)	45,000
Total Net "Expense" for Shelter (after the sale of the house, but ignoring earnings lost on down payment tied up for 30 years in the house and any capital gains tax on the sale of the house)	57,000
Annual Net "Expense" in Owning ($57,000 ÷ 30)	1,900
Monthly Net "Expense" of Owning ($1,900 ÷ 12)	158.33

Thus, it would appear that it would pay for this family to buy the $25,000 house, since the only suitable rental property they can find costs $250 a month to rent. This is about $100 a month more over a period of 30 years, or some $36,000 that this family would seem to save by owning rather than renting, after selling the 30-year-old house. But this exercise ignores any possible earnings that might have resulted if the $4,500 downpayment had been invested for 30 years rather than sunk into the house.

What might such an investment have returned? We can examine this possibility in the example below, where the family rents rather than buys a house.

FINANCIAL PICTURE OF RENTING A HOUSE FOR 30 YEARS

Invests in Stock	$ 4,500
Monthly Rent of	$ 250
Annual Rental ($250 times 12)	3,000
Rental Payment over 30 Years ($3,000 times 30)	$90,000
Minus Estimated Tax Deductions Available to Families Who Rent	0
Total Expenses, after Tax Adjustment	$90,000
Deduct Renter's Equity in House at End of 30 Years	0
Total Outlay for Shelter	$90,000
Deduct Value of $4,500 Invested in Stocks for 30 Years, Assuming the portfolio realizes an 8% annual compound rate of growth (the long-term average on the market)	45,000
Total Net "Expense" for Shelter (ignoring any capital gains tax on the portfolio appreciation if realized)	$45,000
Annual Net "Expenses" in Renting ($45,000 ÷ 30)	1,500
Monthly Net "Expense" in Renting ($1,500 ÷ 12)	125

On the basis of the figures, allowing for the possible portfolio gains from investing the $4,500 rather than using it as a downpayment, it apparently pays to rent rather than own, despite the fact that the renter got no tax benefits nor had any equity in his rented house after 30 years. However, there are two reasons why this may not yet be the right answer.

(1) We have assumed that, when the house is rented, the family can invest their $4,500 and get an average compound rate of 8% in returns over the 30 years. Although computer studies on market prices, going back to 1926, suggest that more or less "random" buying of common stocks, then holding and reinvesting the dividends would result in a return of 8% compounded, let us be more conservative and assume an investment in a savings account, where the gain is only 5%. In this situation, renting would have *cost more.* Gaining 5% in a savings account, the $4,500 would have been worth only

$19,350 at the end of 30 years. As a result, the total net "expense" in renting would have been $70,650 ($90,000 less $19,350) and the monthly "expense" would have been $196.25, as compared with the $158.33 that resulted from owning.

(2) There is yet another reason why renting may not work out favorably for this family. In our example, we have assumed that they were able to rent their house for $250 throughout the entire 30-year period. But, if the $25,000 house appreciated to $45,000 at the end of the 30-year period, it seems more correct to assume similarly that by the end of this period, the family would be paying $450 rather than $250 for their rented house, or an average monthly rental of $350 over 30 years. Once we assume an average monthly rental cost of $350, then the rental payments over 30 years rise to $126,000, well beyond the $90,000 of our initial example, and even if we assume a stock portfolio that appreciates at an 8% rate, total net "expenses" for the 30 years in renting are now $81,000, which send the monthly net "expenses" to $225, as compared with $158.33 in owning.

Now, had the family bought rather than rented, the 30-year mortgage would have protected them from a large share of this inflation in the monthly operating expenses. If we further assume that there is both a rise in the rent and that the initial $4,500 is put in a 5% savings account, the balance tilts even more toward owning, with the higher 30-year expenses from renting ($126,000) now being offset by a terminal value of only $19,350 for the savings account at the end of 30 years, making the monthly net "expense" $296.25 in renting, as compared with $158.33 in owning.

But before letting home ownership take all of the prizes, perhaps you had better consider the following list of major repairs that it appears reasonable to assume might be needed over a 30-year period in a house. Our $300 monthly expense estimate in the example did not allow for complete replacement of any of these items.

Major House Repairs That Are Likely to Cost Over *$1,000*

Major House Repairs That Are Likely to Cost Over $1,000
Replacing the roof
New heating system, if you need ducts
Exterior wood siding
Modernizing a kitchen
Modernizing a bathroom
Replacing a porch, or a frame garage

Note that this list does not include spending to get more rooms or increased convenience—that is, such things as finishing a basement, expanding an attic, adding a room, or building an outdoor swimming pool.

All of these things on the over-$1,000 list above may not happen to your house over 30 years, but they are likely to add a minimum of $5,000 to housing expenditures even if only a few selected repairs on this list become necessary. Of course, it is easy for such repairs to cost much more, and for a $25,000 house, the added cost could increase expenditures by somewhere between 20% and 50% of the $25,000 initial outlay, with much depending on the amount of do-it-yourself that is mixed into the major overhaul jobs. In short, over a 30-year period, these expenditures add somewhere between $15 and $35 a month to the estimated $158.33 net "expense" of owning, thus narrowing the gap between the indicated net "expenses" of renting, under the several assumptions.

What does this add up to?

Many family financial counselors feel that it is a toss-up between renting and owning. In our foregoing examples, this family could have realized a $45,000 nestegg at the end of 30 years either way: as a home-owning family, they would have a house with a $45,000 estimated market value; as renters, they would have a portfolio worth $45,000 in stocks (assuming an 8% appreciation rate on the $4,500 initial investment).

Two additional things, however, may be said about renting vs. owning:

(1) If you think that all you will do with the downpayment is put it in the savings bank and earn a stable 5%, it pays to own instead of rent. However, if you feel you have a safe way to earn more than about 8% a year compounded, it pays to rent and invest the downpayment and all of the upkeep funds that you would have to "feed" into the house over the years.

(2) If a long-term inflation were anticipated even at a fairly moderate rate of 3%, it would probably pay to buy instead of rent. At least part of your regular monthly payments, represented by the mortgage, would be protected against price increases, which is not true of renting. Also, being a debtor, you would be paying off in "cheap" dollars in the later years of your mortgage when the cumulative effects of even a creeping inflation add up.

If owning and renting seem to be running neck and neck from a financial point of view, is there any way to save on shelter? If you decide to rent, it clearly does not pay to attempt to cut corners in the monthly rent payment—low-cost rental property at the present time tends to be slum property, with poor values. And even worse, living in such areas often exposes you to added bodily harm and the expense for protection and insurance, if you can even get the latter. Somewhat more promising might be the prospects for buying a rundown house in a good neighborhood. But with the current fees charged by roofers, plumbers, electricians, and other handy-men in the construction trades, such a house can be made to pay only if you are willing to put a lot of your own time and muscle into the needed repairs.

In the 1970's, then, should you rent or own? As a steady, year-in and year-out prospect, inflationary trends appear more likely than steady, uninterrupted deflation. This would suggest owning your own home.

Deflationary trends, if they come, may prove to be spotty; and construction is one area they might miss. The construction unions maintain rather tight control here and could resist a considerable amount of deflationary pressure from the rest of the economy. This would tend to hold construction costs up, even if there is pronounced weakness in a number of other sectors in the economy. This, in turn, would tend to keep the price of existing housing firm, since much of it could be replaced only at the same, or higher costs. Indeed, lumber prices were one of the places prices continued to rise sharply under Phase II and the early months of Phase III.

Devaluation, even the continuing "devaluation" of flexible exchange rates, would have little effect on housing. Very few building materials are imported—they are too bulky and costly to move. Unless factory-built housing is a new industry of the 1970's (in which case housing might be imported), there seems to be no strategy possible in the 1970's with respect to devaluation that could affect the cost of shelter one way or another. (It might affect fuel costs, but these remain the same whether you rent or buy.)

If you decide to own your own home in the 1970's, you of course will want to shop carefully for the mortgage, getting the best terms available at the time. Hints for finding these better terms will be reviewed in Chapter 6, which is a general survey of the places and terms that can get you extra cash to finance anything from a home to a vacation in Europe.

As a homeowner in the 1970's, there are some other issues that might concern you. For example, you may be concerned about the possibilities that your property might be exposed to hazards that are generally uninsurable, or can be protected under most existing homeowner insurance programs by only limited coverage. Traditionally, homeowners have worried about floods. In the 1950's, many became worried about the chances of nuclear destruction through bombing. In the 1960's, as civil disorder became more commonplace, some homeowners wondered about the consequences of riots. With the exception of floods, exposure to these extraordinary hazards has more to do with proximity to major urban centers than with owning vs. renting. If these hazards really concern you, the only practical thing you can do is to decide to live in a remote, rural area. Suburbia definitely does not qualify as one of the safe havens. To secure maximum protection from these extraordinary hazards, domestic or foreign, you have to be content to work and live well away from the urban areas.

Yet, for the vast majority of American families, removal to remote areas is an impossibility. Over 70% of all Americans now live in or near urban centers, and they usually live there for a good reason—that's where they earn their livelihoods. Some families, however, own two homes—one near their place of employment and another for family retreats and vacations. If your budget can stand the added cost, you might want to consider owning land or a retreat that can provide recreation most of the time and give you a sense of security in the event of a nasty turn in domestic events, or in U.S. relations with the rest of the world. The last time a depression really gripped the U.S., in the 1930's, riots and looting were anticipated by many; but as a matter of fact they never came. And perhaps we will be lucky again, however abrasive the developments of the 1970's become on our patience and nerves. Rural land can make a good investment (see Chapter 10), and if it gives you peace of mind and you can afford it, by all means consider it as a possibility for your family in the 1970's.

The possibility of owning two homes brings up the question of transportation. If you own two homes, with one of them in a remote rural area, you will need a car—especially if you plan to get there in a time of great social unrest. Even with only one home, most U.S. families find a car a necessity, especially with the general decay of public transportation that has occurred in most areas.

There is one major financial problem with owning a car—you can fly to Europe at a cheaper rate per mile than you can drive to the supermarket in your family car! Under the newly approved short-term excursion rates that will take you from New York to London and back for $200, some 7,000 miles both ways, the trip costs a little less than 3 cents a mile. The family automibile costs you about 12 cents a mile to drive if you include depreciation, with this figure rising as the prices at the gasoline pumps rise. If you drive your family car 20,000 miles in a year, that's some $2,400 for transportation.

Only about half of this 12 cents a mile represents direct out-of-pocket costs connected with operating an automobile—gasoline and oil, insurance, maintenance, tires, and license fees. The rest is depreciation, which you can view as the money you should be putting aside to replace your present car when it wears out.

Is there any way to reduce the 12-cents a mile estimate? With a wrench and a manual for repairing your make and model, you may be able to save on the maintenance (saving less than a penny a mile in the 12-cent estimate). You may also be able to defer the day when you have to buy a new car. But these are the only places you can save on transportation.

However, since depreciation accounts for about half the total cost of running your car, you might consider the dollars and cents costs of leasing vs. owning your car. For our example, we will use a new car costing $3,000. A $3,000 car depreciates about 30%, or $900 in the first year, and 17%, or $500 in the second year. If you borrow all of the $3,000 necessary to buy the car, the amount to be paid back over two years, financing will cost you about $360 for the two years. Over two years, then, depreciation and financing will cost you about $1,760 ($900 plus $500 plus $360). This is $73.33 a month over the 24 months. If you can find a two-year leasing contract that will permit you to have use of a car for payment of around $75 a month for two years, you will certainly be no worse off leasing—and you might be better off, depending on how maintenance is handled under the terms of the leasing contract. You could afford to pay an even higher monthly leasing payment if the leasing company carries some of the insurance.

If you plan to pay cash for a new $3,000 car, the leasing company will have to come up with slightly better terms in order for it to pay you to lease. If you pay cash, and draw the money out of a savings account that is paying you 5% compounded, you will lose $307.50 in interest over the two years. Add this to the $1,400 in depreciation over the first two years and your costs are now $1,707.50 for two years, or $71.15 a month over the 24 months.

Of course, if you have been paying more for your cars recently, the leasing company may be able to supply you with transportation that is closer to your expenses here. For instance, if you pay $4,500 for a new car, the first two years of depreciation will be about $1,885 and even self-supplied funds from a savings account will lose you more interest—about $911 over two years. So, with your 2-year expenses now at $2,796, a leasing contract with monthly payments of $112 for 2 years will now pay. You may not get the same class of automobile, but if transportation and saving on transportation are your primary concerns, then it pays to lease.

Having now paid for food, clothing, shelter, and transportation, the only remaining essential expenditure in the family budget is insurance—of the earnings of the family breadwinner, the asset values of the home, the car, and other important family possessions. We discuss insurance in the next chapter.

CHAPTER 4

Reducing Your Risks Through Efficient Insurance Planning

Most American families set aside some of their income to pay the premiums on a variety of insurance policies. The most common forms of insurance protection are against death of the family breadwinner (life insurance), accidents in the family car (automobile insurance), fire and theft in the home (homeowner policies), illness of family members (medical and hospital plans), and inability to pay off installment loans (credit insurance). Although most families planning their own finances feel that some sort of coverage is necessary in these areas, few have clear knowledge about a number of important questions:

(1) How much coverage is enough?
(2) What is the cheapest way to get the amount of coverage I want?
(3) Are my present programs, started in the 1950's and 1960's, adequate for my needs in the 1970's and beyond?

In this chapter, we will develop a framework for answering each of these three questions for the five main types of insurance coverage desired by the average U.S. family—life, auto, home, health, and credit. We will start with life insurance.

(1) *How Much Life Insurance Should I Have in the 1970's?*

Before you shop for life insurance, the very first question you must answer is: How much life insurance should I have? Why not a policy with a $1-million face value? "Why not" becomes quickly evident from the cost of the annual premium, even at age 25, an ordinary life policy for a million dollars has an annual premium of $12,650; as a 20-year endowment from age 25, it is $41,270.

If a $1-million policy is too costly for the average family, what is the absolute minimum amount of life insurance that should be in force on the life of this family's breadwinner? In Chapter 1, we established that the average family's capacity for borrowing was about 3 times its annual pre-tax income. This ratio is thus a good rule-of-thumb minimum for life insurance coverage. The three-to-one rule would make certain that family members left without their income-earner could take care of all the debts and liabilities that might be outstanding and then be able to attack the problems of feeding and clothing themselves without any overhanging burden.

Also, if the family has not borrowed to this theoretical limit, which is most likely, then there will be some funds left over to support the family near its present living standards while they become self-reliant. Using the income levels of Chapter 1, these 3-times-income levels and the costs for ordinary life coverage are shown below:

AVERAGE ANNUAL EARNINGS	3 TIMES COLUMN 1	ANNUAL COST OF ORDINARY LIFE POLICY AT AGE 35
$ 8,000	$24,000	$ 434.16
10,000	30,000	542.70
12,500	37,500	678.38
15,000	45,000	814.05
17,500	52,000	949.73
20,000	60,000	1,085.40
22,500	67,500	1,221.05
25,000	75,000	1,356.75

Another approach in determining how much insurance is needed is to ask how much would be needed to replace the income that would have been earned by the breadwinner in the years following his death. In your own case, you have already estimated the most important figure needed for making this calculation for yourself, by filling out the worksheets in Chapter 1. Go back to these worksheets, pick up the average estimated annual salary and wage line of the What I Expect to Earn table and *multiply* it by the number of years of gainful employment remaining for you. This is done for various income levels below. The table assumes death at age 45 and lists the costs of protecting this lifetime income with ordinary life policy taken out at age 25.

AVERAGE ANNUAL EARNINGS	LIFETIME INCOME LEFT ASSUMING DEATH AT 45	COST OF LIFE POLICY AT AGE 25, ORDINARY LIFE, TO COVER THE REMAINING LIFETIME INCOME
$ 8,000	$160,000	$2,022.40
10,000	200,000	2,528.00
12,500	250,000	3,160.00
15,000	300,000	3,792.00
17,500	350,000	4,424.00
20,000	400,000	5,056.00
22,500	450,000	5,688.00
25,000	500,000	6,320.00

Using ordinary life insurance, it is obviously not cheap to protect either the three-year income or the 20-year income remaining after the death of the breadwinner. Premiums take about 5% of annual before-tax incomes to cover 3-year income protection and around 25% to cover the 20-year incomes. Clearly, covering the remaining 20 years through an ordinary life policy, with 25% of total family income going for premiums, is too costly for most families.

Fortunately, there are cheaper forms of insurance than ordinary life. Ordinary life provides protection *and* a family investment in one package. Life insurance companies also write term insurance, which drops the investment feature and provides only life protection. The difference is that term policies have *no* cash value at any time while they are in force and usually expire at age 65. Coverage of 3-year and 20-year incomes are re-calculated below, assuming that they are covered by level term life insurance, or a policy that provides the same, fixed amount of pure insurance protection throughout the period (or term) during which the policy is in force.

Using level term insurance, the costs of the premiums become relatively more manageable for the average family, which helps explain the spread and popularity of term insurance in recent years, especially as inflation increased the coverage the average family felt it should have. The saving is greatest in providing protection for 3-year incomes of the breadwinner. With a level term policy, it costs the average family only about 1% of their

AVERAGE ANNUAL EARNINGS	3-YEAR COVERAGE, LEVEL TERM CONTRACTED AGE 35	20-YEAR COVERAGE, LEVEL TERM CONTRACTED AGE 25
$ 8,000	$ 84.80	$1,168.00
10,000	106.00	1,460.00
12,500	132.50	1,825.00
15,000	159.00	2,190.00
17,500	185.50	2,415.00
20,000	212.00	2,920.00
22,500	238.50	3,285.00
25,000	265.00	3,650.00

before-tax income, as compared with 5% for an ordinary life policy. Providing protection for the lifetime income of the breadwinner is still somewhat steep, however, taking around 15% of the average family's pre-tax income. Because of its costs, most families do not carry policies that would fully recover the estimated lifetime earnings of the breadwinner. Many families, though, get added protection through yet a third type of insurance, group insurance plans where they work. No figures are shown for group policies since they cannot be taken out by individuals and the rates vary with plans. However, if group insurance is available to your family at work, in professional societies to which family members belong, or through savings banks (available only in some states), the fullest possible use of it should be made to provide protection for the lifetime earnings of the wage earner, since group life insurance is the cheapest form of coverage available.

But you should clearly understand the limitations of both group life insurance and term insurance. Neither builds up any cash surrender value in the policy. This means that the policyholder cannot borrow against these types of policies, and the option to do so is often very advantageous (see Chapter 6). Further, under most plans, term insurance does not provide protection beyond age 65, and group insurance may be even less "dependable" since it terminates when you leave your job (assuming you get it where you work). Even if you are entitled to such a policy through a professional organization (many such organizations have group plans), the insurance protection ends at age 65. For these reasons, most families continue to have private, individual insurance programs of their own, often including some ordinary life insurance along with term and group life insurance.

One point that tends to be neglected in some family life insurance programs is insurance for the wife. If she works, then the family should consider carrying a policy equal to three times her annual take-home pay to protect family living standards. Even if a wife does not work, the husband will have added expenses if there are young children requiring full-time home care in the event of the wife's death. In this case, a life insurance policy equal to at least the estimated 3-year costs of caring for children without a mother should be considered.

Once you have decided on the amounts of life coverage your family needs, you have to make a decision about the best way to meet these indicated coverage needs. Any group coverage in your mix will depend on the place you work, or the availability of group insurance in professional organizations or clubs to which you happen to belong. On your own, your choice will be between ordinary life and some form of term life insurance. If you use all term to age 65, your protection will then end, since the typical term policy does not provide coverage for a policyholder after he reaches the age of 65. If you elect a term life insurance policy, you should understand that all of the premiums paid are for "pure" life protection, there being absolutely no return to you while the policy is in force, except of course to your heirs in the event of death, and absolutely no cash value if you are alive at age 65 and the policy terminates. (Term life insurance works exactly like auto liability insurance, with respect to premiums—neither results in any "cash" value in the policy.) However, if you use ordinary life, you may accept the cash surrender value reached at age 65, or, if you want your heirs to retain a right to the full face value, you must continue to pay premiums. The exact conditions for terminating an ordinary life insurance policy for reasons other than death, or after you have stopped paying premiums, vary slightly from policy to policy, but they are spelled out in great detail in each life insurance policy.

The next table shows the benefits that might result from using either ordinary life or term life to cover family insurance needs of between $24,000 and $75,000 with the policy taken out when the breadwinner is age 35. These are the minimum 3-year income coverages needed by families earning between $8,000 and $25,000 annually. For instance, in the table, a family whose desired life insurance coverage was $45,000, would have to pay $655 a year more to get this protection using ordinary life than if it used term life. Now, if term life were used and the $655 invested each year at a 5% compound rate, this investment would be worth $21,658 at the end of 20 years. On the other hand, if $814 in premiums had been paid each year for ordinary life, this policy would have a cash surrender value of only $14,805 at the end of 20 years. If the policy-holder wanted to retain the claims of his heirs to the higher $45,000 face value of his policy, he would have to continue to pay the $814 annual premium until death terminated the contract.

AMOUNT OF COVERAGE NEEDED FOR 3-YEAR INCOMES	ANNUAL PREMIUMS USING ORDINARY LIFE	ANNUAL PREMIUMS USING TERM LIFE	DIFFERENCE (ORDINARY—TERM PREMIUMS)	INVESTED AT 5% EACH YR. FOR 20 YEARS	CASH VALUE ORDINARY POLICY—END OF 20 YEARS
$24,000	$ 434	$ 85	$ 349	$11,541	$ 7,896
30,000	543	106	437	14,451	9,870
37,500	678	133	545	18,023	12,338
45,000	814	159	655	21,658	14,805
52,500	950	186	764	24,266	17,273
60,000	1,085	212	873	28,860	19,740
67,500	1,221	239	982	32,475	22,208
75,000	1,357	265	1,092	36,112	24,675

This example illustrates clearly why the investment aspects of life insurance itself have not been of much interest to prospective policy-holders in recent years. With greater investment opportunities available to them elsewhere, the return offered by life policies has seemed small and unattractive. Even if the ordinary policy-holder in the example above had decided to continue to pay his $814 in premiums after age 65, then assuming that he had died at age 75, he would have paid $814 for 30 years, or a total of $24,420 in premiums. As a result of this 30-year program, his heirs would have received $45,000 or less than twice the amount of premiums he would have paid. He would have done just about as well by putting the difference in a savings bank each year ($655 in this case) and willing the results of this program ($43,518 after 30 years) to his heirs. If he had lived five more years, to age 80, his heirs would have been happier receiving his savings account—which would have been worth $59,160—rather than his $45,000 face-value life insurance policy.

From these examples, it becomes clear that the best way to secure the coverage your family needs is with term life insurance, for the most part, and banking or investing the difference in the premiums. Your life insurance agent will tell you that this is fine, of course, but then he will ask you: Will you really bank the difference if you are not dunned by the premium notices? If you feel that you might backslide here, you should consider a mix of term and ordinary life, say 80% term and 20% ordinary, depending on how lax you think you might be in making the scheduled annual investments of the premium savings strictly on your own.

How much life insurance coverage will you need in the 1970's and beyond? Inflation is likely to be with us for some time longer. This means that your life insurance needs will be rising to cover your inflated earnings of future years. Even a 3% rate of inflation annually would double your coverage needs in 23½ years. While you can usually *reduce* the amount of life insurance you have without affecting your premium rates per $1,000 of coverage, you can *never increase* your total coverage at an older age without having to pay higher premiums for the additional amount of coverage desired. Therefore, looking ahead, it would be advisable to carry a little more total coverage than you might think you need now, to allow for more inflation in the 1970's. If this expected additional inflation does not come, you can usually reduce the total life insurance you have outstanding, especially if your policy is written in "units."

Deflation in the 1970's, if it reduces rates of return available generally in the economy, will make the investment aspects of life insurance look a little more attractive than they did in the 1950's and 1960's. But even with deflation, it is doubtful that life insurance can offer yields that can compare favorably with those available to an enterprising investor in the 1970's. Whether you decide to opt for ordinary life insurance and its very tame appreciation potentials (2½–3% on average on the funds invested) depends mainly on whether you plan to devote the time and energy required to become a self-reliant investor in the 1970's.

Since your premiums will be collected in U.S. dollars and the benefits under your life insurance contract (any cash surrender value) will be paid to you or your heirs in U.S. dollars, any possible further devaluation will have no effect on the type of contract you decide will best serve your life insurance needs.

(2) *How Much Automobile Insurance Should I Have in the 1970's?*

In most states, you have little choice in your answer—you have to carry a minimum of public liability (bodily injury) coverage before the state will license your motor vehicle. However, you do have a few choices:

(1) You can usually elect to have a $50 or a $100 deductible on your liability coverage. The premiums saved by introducing a $100 deductible are worth the chance that you might have to come up with $50 extra as a result of a collision. Elect the $100 deductible.

(2) You can also choose to supplement your liability coverage with collision coverage, or coverage for the damages on your own car, even in a "one-car" accident. It does not pay to cover collision damages on an older car. Certainly after a car is three years old, it pays to eliminate this coverage.

(3) It might pay to carry more than the minimum for bodily injury coverage. With inflation, juries have been making higher awards. Check the premium differences and the liability laws in the state in which you do most of your driving.

(4) You might want to consider buying auto insurance from a "captive agent" like Allstate. These companies generally are able to charge lower premiums because the agents get less compensation than do the "independent agents." But the captive agent often gives you less service and is less likely to intercede in the case of a disputed claim than is the independent agent. You will have to choose among these differences as a result of your own experiences with the agents in your own local community.

In the 1970's, the most important change that is likely to come in automobile insurance is from the spread of no-fault insurance. In Massachusetts, where no-fault automobile insurance was introduced in January, 1971, policy-holders got a 15% cut in rates when it was introduced. After a year of operation, Massachusetts' Governor Francis W. Sargent has said that an additional 27.6% cut in rates was justified by experience over the year in no-fault car insurance. Other states are considering enacting legislation to introduce no-fault insurance (and some have adopted it) and there is a bill in Congress to adopt a national plan. If a no-fault program is offered in your state, by all means take advantage of the savings offered. The chief advantage you would be losing is the right to sue for alleged pain and suffering as a result of a car accident—and few of these cases result in substantial awards under the old insurance programs, even with its backbreaking annual premiums.

(3) *How Much Homeowners Insurance Should I Have in the 1970's?*

It simply does not pay to cut corners here. For example, suppose your home and its contents are worth $40,000, *excluding the value of the land* (you can't "insure" land—anyway it won't burn). Yet you cover this real property and its contents with a $16,000 policy (40% coverage). Now, suppose you experience a fire, with the damages estimated at $16,000, the value of your policy? You collect the $16,000? Right? *Wrong!* The insurance company will argue that with the house and its contents so obviously under-insured, you were in fact acting as a "co-insurer." Therefore, they will award you—not $16,000 but only $8,000, letting you, the "co-insurer," come up with the other half.

Here is how the co-insurance clause would work for a house valued at $40,000, exclusive of the land:

HOMEOWNERS INSURANCE COVERAGE PURCHASED ON A $40,000 HOUSE	100% ($40,000)	80% ($32,000)	40% ($16,000)	5% ($2,000)
AMOUNT OF LOSS	AMOUNT OF RECOVERY (PAID BY INSURANCE COMPANY)			
$40,000	$40,000	$32,000	$16,000	$2,000
32,000	32,000	32,000	16,000	2,000
16,000	16,000	16,000	8,000	1,000
2,000	2,000	2,000	1,000	125

Policies are generally written over 3 years—an advantage, with coverage costs going up. Rates are generally competitive and fairly standard among insurance companies offering this kind of coverage. Deflation and further devaluation, should they show up in the 1970's, would pose few problems. However, with additional inflation likely in the 1970's, it will pay to conduct periodic reviews to make certain that your coverage is adequate and reflects the value of recent acquisitions and the current market value of your house and construction costs for repairs.

(4) *How Much Health Insurance Should I Have in the 1970's?*

In the inflation of the 1960's and the early 1970's, the costs of medical care generally were at the head of the pack, resulting in a sharp increase in the premiums for all types of medical insurance programs. Most employees have some form of hospital and surgical expense insurance on the job, with many of these programs including some type of major medical or "calamity" coverage. In a time in which premiums have skyrocketed, these plans offer the lowest cost coverage available.

Faced with the higher costs of medical care, some families have decided to add private plans to the base of the health coverage plans they are entitled to on the job. If you do decide you need more health coverage, several pitfalls should be avoided:

(1) Any private plans should be carefully fitted into the health coverage you have on the job. Often, premiums are wasted in private plans since most policies will not pay off twice for claims covered by other plans. Thus, if you do buy private coverage, make certain that it

covers only the *gaps* in your on-the-job health coverage, with no serious overlaps; otherwise, you are wasting premium money.

(2) Some families attempt to cover small medical expenses and regular visits to the doctor with their private plans, since such costs are generally not covered by on-the-job health plans. But these policies are usually very expensive. If your family has an abnormal amount of illnesses, this approach might work; but you should view it more as "prepayment" for expected trips to the doctor rather than "insurance." For most families, efforts to get full coverage in advance is too expensive. Usually, it pays to accept some of the risk through self-insurance—that is, setting aside funds that are earning a return but yet are available to offset unexpectedly large medical bills.

(3) Loss-of-income insurance plans are generally expensive and do not pay off unless the policy-holder is actually hospitalized. With the trend toward shorter hospital stays, which partly reflects the shortage of hospital beds, many of these policies would pay only in extreme cases. For the most part, the premiums are too high in light of the average benefits a policy-holder is likely to receive. Protect your income other ways. Also, most of the loss-of-income insurance plans have "waiting periods"; if you have self-insured yourself here, then there is no waiting period.

(5) *How Much Credit Insurance Should I Have in the 1970's?*

Recently, under the terms of many installment loans you are given little choice—credit insurance is part of the total package and its costs are included in the charges you pay for borrowing money. However, if you are given an option, should you take the credit insurance offered when you enter into a borrowing contract—an installment loan or a mortgage?

Credit insurance is a type of life insurance, and in general, this type of life insurance should cost between 50 cents and $1.00 for each $100 of indebtedness for a 12-month period. (There are exceptions. This insurance is often written on a group basis; therefore, a mobile home or trailer concern that sells mainly to senior citizens will have higher costs for its installment customers.) But there are abuses in this type of insurance. Since the lender typically finds the insurer and since his commission is figured as a percentage of the premium, he of course has little incentive to find a low premium. So if you have an option and the cost appears high, see if you can find term insurance from another source.

In this part of the book, we have reviewed the ways in which you can stretch your dollars and leave more dollars over to support your defensive investment programs for the 1970's. Now, we will investigate safe places to put these money savings until you are ready to commit them to investments in better yielding assets.

Part II

PROTECTING WHAT YOU ARE ABLE TO SAVE

CHAPTER 5

Banks—Can You Trust Them?

You can trust the banks with up to $20,000 of your money if they are members of the Federal Deposit Insurance Corporation (F.D.I.C.)—most are. Beyond that, it's every man for himself.

While this is the major difference between now and the 1930's—there was no such insurance then—you might well ask whether today's insured checking and savings accounts do not just shift the weak point, should any real trouble come, from the member banks to their insuring agency, the F.D.I.C.? In the future, if a number of banks were to get into trouble at the same time, wouldn't this cause a "run" on the F.D.I.C. by all of the depositors? Ever since the F.D.I.C. was established in 1933, there has fortunately been no real test of the system; and admittedly, if bank failures became very widespread, the reserves built up by the F.D.I.C. probably would prove insufficient to provide immediate payment for all banking accounts up to $20,000. However, whatever reserves the F.D.I.C. does have would most likely be used to underwrite short-term borrowing from the Federal Reserve Bank, or even the U.S. Treasury if necessary, until the F.D.I.C could get the crisis in hand and locate the liquid funds to satisfy depositors. Obviously, it would be in the interest of the Federal Reserve and the Treasury to cooperate to the fullest with the F.D.I.C. in the event of serious trouble in the banking system. It appears safe to assume, then, that you would eventually get your money if your account was less than $20,000 and your bank was a member of the F.D.I.C.

But, this does not mean that there might not be temporary inconvenience. Even now when an isolated single bank fails, depositors usually have to wait for their money anywhere from a few days to a few weeks—it takes time for the F.D.I.C to go over the books of a bank in trouble.

If you wish to be spared any possible inconvenience, you might stash away \$200–\$500 in cash. However, holding idle cash does lose you interest—\$200 in 5½% Series E bonds for 5 years would earn you \$61.40 and for 10 years \$141.60. Also there is a problem of finding a safe place to hold \$200–\$500 in cash. Robberies are on the increase in the U.S., so your home is definitely not safe. Safe deposit boxes formerly were thought absolutely secure under all conditions, but bank bombings in the late 1960's and early 1970's have raised some minor doubts about even these havens for valuables. You might consider Swiss banks since they have a long-standing reputation as the ultimate refuge for all fearful investors around the world; but if your objective is to assure ready cash during any possible U.S. banking crisis, you may not have improved your position by putting your cash over 4,000 air-miles away from New York.

Credit cards, such as those issued by American Express and Diners' Club, do offer a practical and relatively inexpensive alternative to holding idle cash against emergencies. These credit cards will cost you \$10 to \$15 for the initiation fee and \$10 each year thereafter and will give you access to a wide variety of goods and services, certainly quite sufficient to tide you over any banking crisis. Of course, the banks themselves issue credit cards, some of them free; but while they are often convenient for shopping in local stores, they might be less acceptable during a banking crisis. In normal times, you might consider having both a credit card issued by a bank and one issued by a nonbanking source; but if there is a confidence crisis in banking, you will probably do better with your American Express or Diners' Club card.

Now, what is the best way to use a bank?

In the modern world, at least a checking account is a must for most families. The objective here is not earnings, of course. In fact, you will pay "negative" interest for the privilege of having a checking account—most banks either charge for checks, or demand minimum balances which must be maintained to avoid charges. Either way, you pay for writing checks, but the added convenience is worth it—the cost of shoe leather, gasoline, and your time connected with paying bills in cash would certainly equal the current charges for maintaining checking accounts.

Savings accounts are another matter. Let's first look at savings accounts in commercial banks (in contrast to savings banks). Such accounts have two objectives: (1) to earn interest and (2) to still have liquidity, that is, a ready source of cash without suffering a loss from the sale of an asset. If you put your money in a common stock, for example, it is true that you may earn more than in a savings account. But although you may be able to sell your stock in a hurry, you may not be able to get what you paid for the stock originally on the quick sale. Therefore, there is a place for a savings account in most families' financial asset mix, to act as a temporary marshaling ground, if nothing else, for your funds until they can be placed at higher yields.

However, if you are putting money away on a longer term basis in a savings account, you can generally earn slightly higher yields at regular savings banks or savings and loan banks than you can at commercial banks. Savings banks and savings and loan banks are generally members of the F.D.I.C., so you get the same protection you do at commercial banks. This feature of insurance makes such passbook savings (in savings and savings and loan banks) slightly more attractive than corporate bonds, even though the bonds may pay higher yields—$1,000 placed in a bond is not insured, while $1,000 in most savings accounts is.

One word of caution about leaving your money long-term in savings accounts of any kind in the 1970's—the interest paid is not fixed. Interest rates were rising on savings accounts during the 1960's and into the 1970's, years generally of money scarcity. But there is nothing that guarantees these interest rates—they can go down in times when money is more plentiful and the banks are less eager to attract loanable funds. In fact, in January 1972, First National City Bank of New York cut the interest it was willing to pay regular savings accounts from 4½% to 4%, the first such cut since 1938.

If you want to nail down the interest rate you are receiving, you will have to buy bonds. Since corporate bonds are not insured, the only way you get an absolutely fixed yield and protection of your principal comparable to that provided by a savings account, is through the purchase of U.S. government Series E bonds. Currently, they yield 5½% and are protected by the ability of the Federal government to tax or, as a last resort, to print money to pay them off. Series E bonds were long neglected by investors because of the sharp inflation of the 1950's and 1960's which tended to offset the lower interest rates then offered by these bonds—as low as 3¼% in earlier years. But now that Series E bonds yield 5½% and inflation is expected to average closer to a 3–4% rate, many investors are once again considering them as at least temporary resting places for their idle funds. Although somewhat less convenient than a savings account, they can usually be cashed in on short notice at any bank for the initial amount invested plus accumulated interest.

Within the borders of the U.S., then, the best resting places for temporarily idle funds in the '70's would appear to be (1) checking accounts at commercial banks, chiefly for convenience; (2) savings accounts at savings banks or savings and loan banks, chiefly for liquidity plus some yield; and (3) U.S. government Series E bonds, for the best available yield, safety, and liquidity (assuming *all* three are desired at the same time).

Outside the borders of the U.S., there is the possibility of a savings account in a Swiss bank. As we have noted above, such an account offers little protection in the event of a cash crisis following a round of U.S. bank failures, but such an account can offer defense over the longer haul. This leaves us with another question: Can you trust a Swiss banker?

He is discreet. He will pay you interest on your account (between 4% and 5%). Your money will be in Swiss francs, a currency that has a long record of stability, and even if further devaluation comes in the 1970's, the Swiss franc is likely to suffer the least in terms of loss in international exchange value. If deflation comes, your Swiss account will be worth more and be secure. If there is further world-wide inflation in the 1970's, you are likely to suffer less with your money in Swiss francs than you might in U.S. or some other currencies.

There are drawbacks. Although your Swiss banker may be discreet, you will also find that he is "distant" in several senses of the word. There are over 4,000 airmiles separating you and him, but there is also some reluctance on the part of these banks to encourage accounts from abroad, especially from the U.S. After all, the Swiss, like all other West European countries, are swimming in U.S. dollar claims, so why do they need more, especially in the form of thousands of small accounts that cost more to open and supervise than do large accounts? If the funds you have to place in a Swiss bank are relatively small, less than $50,000, you may find that your overtures will be met with less than enthusiasm. However, air mail postage to Switzerland is 21¢ for half an ounce. So you can easily correspond with three or four Swiss banks to check out the likelihood of opening a Swiss franc deposit account in one of them. You can get their addresses out of the American Bankers Association's international directory of banks. (Such a move would make even more sense if you think that at any time in the future you might wish to live abroad—see Chapter 20.)

Regardless of where you decide to place your idle cash awaiting the right investment and the right time for committing your funds, you will also want to know the sources and the costs of adding to your funds through borrowing. The places the average family can borrow most readily at the present time and into the 1970's are briefly surveyed next.

CHAPTER 6

Borrowing—Using Other People's Money to Make Money

Willie Sutton, the noted bank robber, was once asked why he robbed banks. His reply was direct and to the point: "Because that's where the money is."

You might follow this logic when you borrow. Generally, if you borrow from a non-bank source such as a finance company, they will go to the bank, borrow the money and then lend it to you. So why not eliminate the middleman and his profit by going directly to the source? As a rule, it generally pays to check the amounts and terms you can get from a commercial bank before you explore other sources for borrowing.

But as with most rules, there are exceptions. From some sources you may be able to get money cheaper than you can at the bank—for example, at no cost on a 30-day charge account at a department store, or by borrowing against the cash surrender value of your ordinary life insurance.

At other times, it is not the costs but the amounts that will make you investigate non-bank sources for borrowing. While bankers may be in a position to loan under better terms than most lenders, they are not always willing to let you have as much as you would like. In this case, you will have to shop around, even though you know you will most likely pay more for the money. How much more you should be willing to pay will depend, of course, on what you plan to do with the money. If you plan to blow it on a vacation trip to Sun Valley, then narrow financial considerations may not apply. However, if you plan to put the money to work earning other money, there is a basic rule to follow: to justify the assumption of an added debt burden, the expected return, after allowing for the risk, should exceed the cost of borrowing by a good healthy margin.

In this chapter we will make a systematic survey of the possible sources for borrowing generally available to the average U.S. family. These borrowing sources will be considered in order, starting first with the cheapest sources. When the costs are similar, the borrowing sources will be listed in order of the ease, risk and special features for the borrowers, starting with those providing the best non-cost terms to the borrower.

(1) *30-Day Charge Accounts—Costs: 0%; after 30 days, 18%**

Formerly, you had longer to pay without being slapped with charges. But even under current conditions you can extend the length of your free ride. Notice when your bill is closed and sent each month; then, bunch your purchases in the week following the closing of your account for the month—you won't have to pay for 20–30 days after these purchases are made. If you do not pay within the time limits stated on your bill, the department store or oil company will, typically, charge you at an annual rate of 18% to carry you.

(2) *Credit Cards—Costs: 0%; after 30 days, 18%*

Similar to charge accounts (see above). Still, you can do a lot of things now and pay later without paying any interest charges, as long as you pay within the time limits stated on your bill.

(3) *Friends and Relatives—Costs: 0% to more than you will want to pay*

Sometimes you can get by with a little help from your friends and/or relatives. Occasionally, they will charge you nothing but aggravation, which can be plenty. If you do borrow from these sources, it may be best in the long-run to select one of the standard interest plans and agree to pay your friend or relative the same amount—this keeps down possible misunderstandings.

* The interest rates given will be annual rates.

(4) *Cash Surrender Value of Ordinary Life Policy—Costs: 5%*

One advantage of ordinary life insurance (see Chapter 4) is that you have the right to borrow up to 95% of the cash surrender value that has been built up in the policy at the time, with no questions or any credit check whatsoever. You do not have to tell the insurance company what you plan to do with the money, as is the case with a loan at a commercial bank. Check your policy—it will tell you the current cash surrender value and the amount of interest you will have to pay if you borrow. If you have paid-up GI insurance, you can borrow at 4%.

(5) *Passbook Loans at Savings Banks—Costs: 5.6% common*

You surrender your passbook and the bank will loan you an amount up to the amount you have on deposit. Added feature: you get to keep earning the interest, which offsets the interest you are paying, reducing the net cost of this type of borrowing even more. You do not have to go to the savings bank in which you have your passbook account; almost any bank will lend on the same terms against your passbook. You can make further savings by paying back early.

(6) *Home Improvement Loans—Costs: Variable, but FHA-backed loans are occasionally available at 5¾%*

FHA guaranteed loans for home improvement are available at attractive rates, but of course you must start the project before the bank will give you the money. This condition for getting the loan means that you cannot use these funds for other purposes. But getting the loan will help free some of your other funds while your family is making this costly outlay. There is a limit to the amount you can borrow for this purpose under an FHA loan: $5,000.

(7) *Home Mortgages—Costs: 7%–8%, in most of country*

These costs have risen considerably in recent years, mortgage rates of 9½% and higher being reported in various parts of the country. Still, they are cheaper than many types of credit commonly used by families—for example, see item 11, installment loans. Since these rates are generally lower than most families can get elsewhere, some families with large equities built up in their homes have refinanced their mortgages—borrowing against the built-up equity and using the freed funds to purchase other things like automobiles and appliances, or even vacation trips. (Refinancing is *not* a second mortgage—see item 14 below.) Some mortgages are "open-end," meaning that the mortgage (amount loaned) can be added to regularly without red-tape or an increase in the cost. If mortgage rates were to slide in the 1970's, many families who bought their homes when rates were higher—8% or above—will find that they can re-finance their homes at lower rates (a saving in itself) and still have extra funds left over for other investing or spending, unless of course their existing mortgages have stiff penalty clauses for pre-payment.

(8) *Margin Loans at Brokers—Costs: Variable, tied to "call money" rates*

If you borrow to buy stocks, your broker, acting as a middleman, will borrow "call money" from a commercial bank and lend it to you. By law, he must charge at least ½% more than the call rate. Many brokers charge as much as 2% more, especially for small accounts. In early 1974, with the call money rates at around 9½%, the charges from the broker would have been between 10% and 11½%. In early 1973, because call rates were lower, margin borrowing cost between 7 and 8½%.

(9) *Single-Payment Loans at Banks—Costs: Variable*

Charges made by commercial banks for single-payment signature loans, with no collateral, vary with (a) business conditions and (b) the credit-rating of the potential borrower or the borrower's standing with the bank. Commercial banks (and savings banks in some states) also make installment loans (see 11, below), but if you can obtain a single-payment signature loan you will generally get lower rates than with installment loans, even at banks. Banks have a "prime" rate, to which they add points depending on how they view the lender and the riskiness of loaning him money. Recently, this type of borrowing (up to about 10% of the borrower's after-tax income) was available at between 8–15%, depending on credit standing. To establish a standing with a bank, you may wish to borrow small sums, even if you do not need them, raising the amount you ask for each time. This helps establish a source for borrowing at favorable rates when you really need it.

(10) *Credit Unions—Costs: 12%, with lower rates available if you pay back fast*

Credit unions are usually able to provide money cheaper than are other sources for buying such things as automobiles and appliances. Since most credit unions welcome fast pay-back, you can even reduce these costs by paying back the principal ahead of schedule. However, you must be a member of a credit union before you can borrow from it.

(11) *Installment Loans—Costs: Variable, 12–30% common*

Although many U.S. families make use of installment loans to buy big-ticket appliances, television sets, and automobiles, the costs are not usually cheap. Banks have been making more of these loans over the last decade, and appliance and auto dealers generally make them available to their customers. Shop carefully, and give serious consideration to paying cash—the interest you will lose is generally not half as painful as the interest you will be paying. However, since the interest paid is a tax deduction, after allowance for the tax-credit earned, the effective cost of borrowing may be lower if you are in a higher Federal income tax bracket.

(12) *Small Loan Companies—Costs: 24–36% are common*

Avoid if at all possible. The costs are high and these lenders have little to gain by helping you have the courage to pay down your debts and get clear. If you cannot avoid this type of borrowing, then by all means reject any offers to "re-finance" your loan after you have paid down a sizable chunk of it; otherwise, you are hooked.

(13) *Pawnbrokers—Costs: 24–36% in some areas*

For one reason or another, this is one type of lender that did not make it to suburban shopping centers, but if you have access to urban centers, where most of the pawnbrokers have their businesses, you might consider him as an alternative to the small loan company. Often, his costs are about the same as the small loan company, but remember—you owe the pawnbroker nothing unless you actually redeem the article pawned. He will take diamonds, TV sets, binoculars, cameras, radios, typewriters, musical instruments, furs, electric razors, even clothing. Perhaps you have some of these things lying around, they no longer seem essential in your life plans, and it is too much bother to advertise and sell them. Why not pawn them? It will be money found, and you need not pay a cent unless you redeem the article.

(14) *Second Mortgages—Costs: Variable, but 30–40% is not uncommon, after all costs*

Some families have made use of second mortgages in recent years because they were unable to get big enough first mortgages (plus down payments) to cover the inflated prices of the house they wished to purchase. While such resort to second mortgages was understandable, it can hardly be judged as wise from a narrow financial viewpoint. Second mortgages generally must be paid back in much shorter time spans than first mortgages (usually 5 years or less) and the expenses are generally high. With both the expenses and the monthly payment of the principal extremely high, most families who assume these excessive financial burdens run a great risk of losing their homes—even a minor illness or short lay-off of the breadwinner can make these high monthly payments unsupportable. While you might consider re-financing your first mortgage to free the equity you have locked up in your home, *never* take a second mortgage to free cash. Second mortgages are one of the riskiest and most costly methods of financing available to the average family.

(15) *Loan Sharks—Costs: 6-for-5 forever, or more than you will want to pay*

Despite repeated warnings, some families borrow money from "off-beat" sources, usually in their own neighborhoods. Rates are usually exorbitant —you borrow $50 this week, you pay back $60 next week. That's 20% for borrowing money for one week. That is equivalent to over 1,000% at an annual rate, so almost anything is preferable. Still, some people do it; but you *should not* in the 1970's, or in *any* decade.

These fifteen sources, then, are the ones most commonly used by the average U.S. family to stretch their spending power through borrowing. As we have seen, some of these sources offer credit at reasonable rates and on reasonable terms, while some do not and should be avoided for the most part. Whether your family actually should make use of any of these sources of borrowing, however reasonable the costs and the terms, is a question that can be decided only on a case-by-case approach, with each case being decided on its own merits at the time.

In Parts III through V—which review investment opportunities likely to be present in the 1970's—recommendations will be made for the use of borrowing (or leverage, as it is called), wherever it would seem to add greatly to the potentials in a situation without unduly increasing the risks. Many investors have used leverage, or the greater investing power that comes from borrowing extra funds, to improve the results realized from their investment programs in the past. In Parts III through V, we will explore the potentials *and the risks* that might come from using leverage to increase your family's net worth in the '70's and beyond.

There is one further advantage to using any of the fifteen sources of borrowed funds that have been reviewed—namely, that in most cases interest paid can be used as a tax deduction, thereby lowering the effective costs of borrowing by the amount of the tax that is saved. This is only one type of tax-saving that can come from a family investment program. Others are reviewed in the next chapter.

CHAPTER 7

Taxes—How to Avoid or Postpone Them

If you don't pay your taxes, you can go to jail. If you avoid taxes, you have more left over to spend or invest. If you postpone taxes, you have more left over to spend and invest this year.

One way to avoid taxes is to avoid earned income in the year, a perhaps short-sighted approach to your tax problem. Another happier solution might occur to you—avoid *reporting* income for the year. While this is at least a more palatable approach, it has its limits and its jail terms. Most of the income payments you receive are keyed with your Social Security number and flagged to the Internal Revenue Service, so you must report them. This includes wages and salaries, interest on your savings accounts, bonds, and other fixed-income investments, and dividends on your stock.

However, you get some help with stock dividends. You are permitted to exclude the first $100 of dividends from income for tax purposes, or the first $200 when filing a joint return if the stock is owned jointly with your wife (or enough is in her name to earn $100 in cash dividends).

With other income—chiefly income resulting from the sale of assets—you have some options. If the asset has been held for less than six months, you have to declare any gains resulting from its sale as ordinary income, subject to the regular tax rates. However, if the asset is held for longer than six months, you are allowed to count this as capital gains and pay at a reduced rate, regardless of what your marginal tax rate is.

While this capital gains tax shelter is a boon to the investor in stocks and other types of assets, such as land, commodities, and other real property, it often results in an unwise buy or sell decision in an attempt to establish a tax position. As a general rule, your assets, whether they are stocks or real property, should be sold or bought when their markets dictate, not when your tax position says. *Never let a tax consideration interfere with a sensible market move.* Take advantage of the capital gains tax, but do not postpone a sale because of it—the profits may not be there to tax the next time you try to sell.

Often, it pays to review your income in the month of December, checking whether there are fees and income owed you that might be postponed, or speeded up, depending on whether you can afford more taxable income in the present year or your tax situation would be enhanced if this income could be deferred. Of course, we are talking about shifts of about a month—between December of one year and January of the following. Any more distant moves might be unwise—if you postpone fees too far forward, there is a greater chance you may never receive them to pay taxes on.

After you have estimated your earned income and the income you have received from the purchase and sale of assets in the year, you are in a position to add up your deductions. The location of legitimate deductions that will satisfy the IRS tax collectors is the chief way through which most families reduce their tax bill. You will probably want to examine carefully the suggestions contained in some of the tax guides that are available on the newsstands or in the bookstores, or you may wish to consult with a tax accountant if your potential deductions are both numerous and appear to be interesting special instances of the usual allowable deductions spelled out in these manuals.

There have been no fundamental changes over the past few years in the types of deductions that the average family may take. Some general observations might be made about the deductions that most families find most useful.

Personal exemptions are probably the most important single deduction for most families, and they are now $750 for each family member and dependent.

Other important tax considerations:

> With medical expenses taking 6–8% of the average family budget (see Chapter 2), more families are finding it worthwhile to go through the rather elaborate calculations necessary to take the more than 1% limit of adjusted gross income in medications and the 3% deduction for medical expenses, including health insurance.

- As local property and school taxes have risen, the tax advantages of home ownership have been strengthened in recent years.
- If you want to find out the tax advantage of owning a municipal bond whose interest is exempt from Federal income tax, use the following formula:

$$T = \frac{E}{1-B}$$

With

E = the interest rate paid on the tax-exempt security

B = your tax bracket

T = interest you would have to earn on a taxable bond to be as well off, after taxes

Suppose you have a tax-exempt bond yielding 6% and that you are in the 35% tax bracket; then substituting in the formula, you have:

$$T = \frac{.06}{1-.35} \quad \text{OR } 9.22\%$$

This means that you would have to earn at least 9.22% on a corporate bond to keep 6%, after taxes, if you were in the 35% tax bracket (your marginal tax rate is 35%). This explains why many wealthy investors are partial to tax-exempts in their portfolios.*

In addition to saving through proper preparation of your current income tax returns, you will also want to give some consideration to the tax aspects of planning for your retirement and the tax aspects of estate planning in general. From a tax point of view, any realized income that you can shift to your retirement years will be beneficial since you will no longer be reporting earned income. These earnings thus will be placed in lower tax brackets, even though they may be ordinary income. You may wish to seek expert tax

* You might also note that the average cash dividends on a common stock would also have to be in excess of 9.22% to attract this investor in the 35% tax bracket on the basis of yield. Of course, if he anticipated a handsome capital gains from the sale of this common stock, which would be tax-sheltered, he might be willing to pay more for the common and thereby accept a lower current yield. Common stocks are discussed more fully in Chapter 14.

or legal counsel in designing both your retirement and your estate programs.

While tax considerations can be important, they should always be kept in perspective—far more important is having an income to tax or an estate to plan. We have cleared up some matters of family budgeting in Part I and some details about handling the funds you are able to earn and save in Part II. Now, in the remaining chapters, we are in a position to explore ways of increasing your total income and building a larger net worth, or an estate, for your family in the 1970's and beyond.

Part III

HOW TO BEGIN MAKING EXTRA MONEY— LOW-RISK INVESTMENTS

CHAPTER 8

First Things First—Taking Care of Today

Before you can buy a stake in tomorrow, you have to nail down today. There are two things your family needs now, before you attempt to send some of your current income forward to add to your spending power in future years, namely:

(1) *Cash reserves,* to guard against temporary interruptions in the family's present earnings.
(2) *Life insurance,* to guard against a permanent loss of the breadwinner's earnings.

In Chapters 1 and 4 we have developed some general principles for determining the necessary levels of cash reserves and life insurance for the average family. Now we will review these needs and establish targets for the 1970's.

In the examples of Chapter 1, we assumed that an absolute minimum of three months in wages and salaries had been set aside by our families and held in the form of cash reserves. This was a minimum—most family counselors advise a larger cash reserve for greater family security. So, for cash reserves we will follow the *six-months rule.* A set-aside of at least six months of average monthly earnings in the family wages and salary (husband and wife, if they both work) should be sufficient to act as a first line of defense in emergencies—a layoff or illness of one or more of the family breadwinners, etc.

As an absolute *minimum* in life insurance needs, we used in Chapter 4 *three years of annual wages and salaries,* with the reasons for adopting this minimum given in that chapter. Upward limits for life insurance needs were set by the expected lifetime incomes remaining to the family breadwinners. However, this maximal coverage was shown to be far too expensive for the average family, with actual life insurance coverage recommended to fall somewhere between the minimum of 3 years of annual income and the complete protection of the remaining lifetime income.

What is the optimum amount of life insurance coverage between this minimum, which is probably too low, and complete lifetime coverage, which is too expensive? Most families' counselors say that at least five years of annual wages and salaries should be covered by life insurance, assuming that the home mortgage is covered separately by a group term life policy and that any large family loans are also covered by credit life insurance, or other coverages. If the big blocks of family borrowing are not covered by policies, then enough life insurance to cover the average monthly payments on these borrowings should be *added* to the 5-year annual wage and salary total. Here we will assume that the family debt is covered by separate policies, and adopt the *5-year rule* for life insurance coverage.

Using the 6-month rule for cash reserves and the 5-year rule for life insurance coverage, we can set targets for family financial planning. This is done for incomes in the $8,000 to $25,000 ranges in the table below.

AVERAGE ANNUAL EARNINGS	CASH RESERVES 6-MONTH RULE	EARNINGS ON CASH AT 5%	LIFE INSURANCE 5-YEAR RULE	PREMIUMS ON LEVEL TERM LIFE	
				AGE 25	AGE 35
$ 8,000	$ 4,000	$200	$ 40,000	$292	$ 424
10,000	5,000	250	50,000	365	530
12,500	6,250	313	62,500	456	663
15,000	7,500	375	75,000	548	795
17,500	8,750	438	87,500	639	928
20,000	10,000	500	100,000	730	1,060
22,500	11,250	562	112,500	821	1,193
25,000	12,500	624	125,000	913	1,325

In the 1970's, in what form should the cash reserves be held, and how should the indicated life insurance coverages be met?

· *Implementing the 6-Month Rule for Cash Reserves:* Hold 50% in savings accounts, certificates of deposit, long-term (2-year) accounts at banks, all of which have current earned interest available in the 5–6% range. Since some of these interest rates currently being paid may weaken at various times in the 1970's, hold 50% of your cash reserves in the form of U.S. government Series E bonds, which contracts to provide a 5½% rate of return if held to maturity.

· *Implementing the 5-Year Rule for Life Insurance*: Keep 100% of your program in level term life insurance—or group life insurance programs available through professional groups or other organizations *not* connected with your place of employment—and *bank the savings,* that is, the difference between the lower term life and the higher ordinary life premiums (see Chapter 4). *Do not* include group insurance programs at your place of employment in implementing the 5-year rule—you may change jobs and lose this protection. If you feel that you will be unable to maintain a program of banking the savings from the premiums of term versus ordinary life, consider some mix of term and ordinary life in reaching your coverage target, say 80% term and 20% ordinary, or even 50/50 if you feel that you will backslide regularly.

What if your current cash reserves and insurance programs do not meet the limits established by the 6-month rule and the 5-year rule? Then it is a first priority of your financial program to bring your cash reserves and life insurance program up to these levels. Adopt immediately the *10% rule for freeing cash.* Under this 10% rule, you take 10% of your weekly, monthly, or annual before-tax earnings immediately off the top upon receipt, freeing them for use in your family financial program. If your cash reserves and life insurance programs are below target, funds freed under the 10% rule are channeled into these areas until they are up to proper level.

· *Implementing the 10% Rule for Freeing Cash:* First, put 10% of each paycheck immediately into a special savings account. Second, estimate the taxes being withheld in the current year and put 10% of this amount also into this special savings account. These two steps will have freed 10% of your before-tax income. If this 10% set-aside pinches and makes it difficult for your family to meet its regular monthly bills, then review your family budget—especially the What I Plan to Spend Each Month table in Chapter 1, and find places you can cut.

· *Implementing the 10% Rule for Freeing More Cash:* If you have been able to live with the 10% rule, flat, then you might want to try for additional free cash funds. In this case, simply add 1% to the amount you take off the top of every other paycheck—11%, 12%, 13%, etc. Note the effects on your family's living style. When it really hurts and you can find no more places to cut, you will have reached your family's capacity limit for freeing cash. This procedure is far simpler to put into practice than the conventional budgeting games many families play: putting $1.73 in an envelope each week for entertainment, $5.75 each week for vacations, etc. With less working cash each week after taking out the 10% plus, your family can attempt to adjust their living standards with complete flexibility to choose in practice where the cuts will come, week by week. Since you are banking the 10% plus, there will be no serious damage done if the amounts of cash you are attempting to free prove too ambitious. You can always retreat by withdrawing cash and, with the next paycheck, reducing by 1% the level of 10% plus you have reached.

As these cash funds are freed and accumulate in the special savings account, you should begin to make plans for committing them. At first, of course, these freed cash funds should be used to build up cash reserves under the 6-month rule and life insurance coverage under the 5-year rule. But once these targets are reached, you are in a position to use these freed cash funds to acquire other types of assets for your family—assets that will add to family security later in the 1970's and increase your family's net worth going into the 1980's. In the remaining chapters of Part III, low-risk opportunities for using freed cash, over and above the cash needed for reserves and life insurance, will be discussed. In Parts IV and V, more aggressive uses will be suggested for the funds freed under the 10% rule.

CHAPTER 9

Buying Bonds—Getting the Real Gold from the Gilt-Edged

Most bonds come in one standard size, being issued in $1,000 denominations. There are some exceptions. Series E bonds issued by the Federal government come in a variety of smaller sizes, starting at the $18.75 level. However, the Series H bonds, also issued by the Federal government, are standard $1,000 bonds. On rare occasions, a corporation will issue a "junior" bond in a $100 denomination. But, for the most part, the $1,000 bond is the rule.

All bonds are formal I.O.U.'s of the issuer. They promise to pay the holder a fixed, annual amount of interest (called the coupon or yield) until the amount lent by the bondholder (called, variously, the principal, the face value of the bond, or the par value of the bond) is paid back (the bond is redeemed or matures). If the issuer fails to meet any of the obligations under the terms of the bond, the bond is in default and the issuer is in bankruptcy. Bonds are issued (stay in force) for a fixed number of years, often twenty years, the only exception being a consul which has no redemption date. For all practical purposes you can forget about consuls since none exists in the U.S.

With all bonds having the same basic features, regardless of issuer, the chief distinction of importance, aside from the amount of interest promised, is the credit rating and financial strength of the issuer or, stated negatively, the chance that the issuer will default. In this respect, the bonds issued by the U.S. government are considered to be among the safest and soundest in the world. Few would question the ability of the U.S. government to meet its obligations under the terms of the bonds it issues. For one thing, it has the power to tax one of the wealthiest economies in the world to raise the needed interest payments and funds necessary to redeem the bonds when they mature. And the Federal government has an impressive back-up power—the legal right under the Constitution to print paper money if the ability to tax were to waver. So, Series E savings bonds and Series H standard bonds issued by the Federal government are considered the lowest risk bonds available to investors in the U.S.

Municipal bonds—issued by state governments, cities, school districts, and all types of local governmental units with taxing power—are considered slightly more risky than U.S. government issues. While all of these issuers have the power to tax, their willingness and ability to tax may be subject to more grassroot pressures and resistance than is the case with the Federal government. Also, none of these governmental units has the last resort power to print paper money to meet its obligations if all else fails. However, municipal bonds have one special feature of interest to some investors—the interest they pay is not subject to the Federal income tax.

Corporations have neither the power to tax nor print paper money to meet their obligations under the terms of the bonds they issue. Whether a corporate bond will be redeemed depends, ultimately, on whether the corporation is selling a line of products that the public considers essential, whether its customers feel it is doing a good job in satisfying these basic needs, and whether the corporation can make money at it. Companies doing a good job selling bread might be considered a good risk, if they had been doing it for a number of years. A company whose exclusive business is selling hula hoops might be considered a poor risk for the long haul.

Still, you do not have to be particularly astute to buy bonds. There are only five essential bits of information you need:

(1) The selling price of the bond at the moment.
(2) The dollar amount of interest you will be paid each year.
(3) The number of years you will get this interest—years to maturity.
(4) The amount you will get back when the bond matures.
(5) The chances that the company will not be able to pay off at maturity.

Anything else you might happen to know about the bond or its issuer is beside the point.

All five of these essential bits of information about a bond are quite easy to find. For example, you can find out the selling price, the annual interest you will be paid, years to maturity, and the amount you will get back at maturity simply by looking in a daily newspaper that carries a table of bond quotations. A typical quotation looks like this:

BONDS	CURRENT YIELD	SALES IN $1,000	HIGH	LOW	LAST	NET CHANGE
ATT 6½s79	6.7	16	96¼	96	96¼	+½

• *Finding the Selling Price:* Bonds are quoted in the 100's. For example, if a bond is quoted at 100, this means that you will have to pay $1,000 to acquire it. In the quotation shown above, the bond closed at 96¼, meaning at a price of $962.50. If the quote is 33, you pay $330. A quote of 112 means you pay $1,120; 77½ means you pay $775. Rule: *Multiply the bond quote by 10 to find the selling price.*

• *Finding the Interest:* After the name of the bond, there will appear a figure, such as 6½s, as in the example.* This is the percentage of the par value, or interest, that the holder of the bond will receive each year. Par for almost all bonds is $1,000, the amount that the person holding the bond will get when it matures and the base on which the stated yield is calculated. If the stated yield is 6½s, this means that the holder will receive 6½% of the $1,000 par, or $65. If the yield is 8⅞%, this can be expressed as a decimal fraction .08875, which when multiplied by $1,000 gives $88.75, the annual amount of interest. Rule: *Multiply the yield, expressed as a decimal fraction, by $1,000 to find the amount you will receive annually in interest.*

• *Finding the Years to Maturity:* After the first figure, there will be another, such as 79, as in the example. This is the year the bond will be paid back—in this case 1979. If the bond is to be paid back after the year 2000, the table will carry the full date, for example, 2011. To find the number of years to maturity subtract the present year from the year of maturity—1979 − 1974 = 5. If the bond has already paid its interest in the current year (you will have to look this up in a bond manual in your local library, or ask your broker), then this is the number of interest payments you can expect. If it has not paid its annual interest as yet, then add 1 to this number. Rule: *To find the number of years to maturity subtract the current year from the maturity year, then add 1 if the current year's interest has not been paid.*

• *Finding How Much the Bond Will Pay at Maturity:* If the bond you are

* If you are puzzled by the "s," it simply reproduces the speech patterns of bond dealers: "ATT six and a half's" becomes "6½s."

interested in is quoted in a local newspaper's bond table with no indication that there is a special par value, you can assume that you will receive $1,000 at maturity. However, before you actually buy the bond, you should look up the bond in a manual, or ask your broker. Rule: *Assume a payback of $1,000, unless stated to the contrary.*

· *Other Information in Bond Quotation Listings.* Some local newspapers have recently been including current yields for bonds in their quotation listings. This current yield is the yield based on the prices that the bond has been selling at in recent trading days. However, this yield *is not necessarily* the yield based on the *current* day's trading range. For instance, in our example the ATT 6½s pay a coupon of $65. At the low for the day, 96, this would be a yield of 6.77%, not the 6.7% cited as the "current yield." At its high and close for the day, 96¼, the indicated yield would be 6.75%, which is still slightly more than the 6.7% given as the current yield. So, these current yield figures, while providing useful additional information about the bond, should not be used uncritically in your analysis.

In sum, what can you find out from a listing of bond quotations in a local newspaper? In our example of the ATT bonds, for instance, we found out that we would have to pay somewhere between $960 and $962.50 to purchase one of these bonds currently. If we held it until 1979, it would mature and we would receive $1,000, or between $37.50 and $40 more than we paid for it. Even if further investigation reveals that the ATT 6½s79 has already paid its coupon for 1974, if we now buy and hold one bond to maturity we will receive $65 a year for five years—1975, 1976, 1977, 1978, and 1979, or a total of $325. So, the maximum benefit possible from buying the bond lies between $362.50 and $365.00, the $37.50 to $40 potential capital gains when the bond matures (depending upon the actual purchase price) plus the annual interest payments of $65, or $325 for five years (assuming the 1974 coupon has already been paid).

This is about as far as you can go with the bond quotation table in the daily newspaper. To find out the fifth essential bit of information about a bond—the risk factor—you will have to consult either the *Standard & Poor's* or *Moody's* bond manuals. These manuals, or the essential information from them, are usually available in the public library. If not, try your bank or brokerage office.

· *Measuring the Likelihood that a Bond Will Pay Off the Principal at Maturity:* In some ways, this is the most critical factor concerning your decision to buy a bond. Clearly, you would think twice about buying a bond that yields 10% on its $1,000 par value, or $100 a year, even if it were available at a steep discount, say \$800, where its \$100 coupon would yield you 12.5%, if you felt there was a good chance that the company might go bankrupt and the bond be defaulted. Even if the bond only had five years to maturity, you would hesitate if the chances of default were high. In fact, if you had been able to buy a bond maturing in five years for \$800, part of the reason you bought the bond would have been the assumption that you would receive the full \$1,000 par value when the bond matured. This assumption is so well established that bonds are usually quoted in terms of their "yields to maturity," a calculation that uses both the annual interest payment and the appreciation potential in a bond in arriving at a measure of the benefits to be gained by buying the bond now and holding it to maturity. The yield to maturity is calculated by taking the sum of annual cash interest payments *plus* the appreciation between the purchase price and the par value, and dividing by the current selling price. This arithmetic gets rather involved, but fortunately there are standard yield-to-maturity interest tables that do all of the calculating work for you. You can find yield-to-maturity by consulting one of these tables, looking up the current quotation in a bond manual, or asking a broker.

But the details of calculating yield-to-maturity are unimportant compared with the question of whether a bond will in fact default at any time you might be holding it. "Familiar" names do not help here (Penn-Central was well-enough known to most investors). It is the cash flow that the company is able to generate that will determine whether it can pay off both its regular annual interest payments and the principal at the time of maturity.

For this, you may want to look at a company's current accounting statements yourself, in order to establish whether it appears able to generate enough cash from operations to pay off its bond holders. Remember that even if the company is treating its stockholders rather shabbily, this need not concern you as a potential bond holder, as long as the company appears capable of generating enough cash flows to pay off its debts.

If you do not feel competent to read and interpret a company's accounting statements, you can make use of the quality ratings of bonds provided by *Standard & Poor's* and *Moody's.* Thousands of bonds are given ratings, in terms of their indicated ability to pay back debt. The ratings are given by a panel of financial experts employed by these two investment advisory services.

Their similar rating systems are summarized on the next page. The ratings go from the best to the worst.

	MOODY'S	STANDARD & POOR'S
High-grade		
Gilt-Edged	Aaa	AAA
High Quality	Aa	AA
Medium-grade		
Highest	A	A
Lower	Baa	BBB
Lowest	Ba	BB
Speculative		
Moderately	B	B
Very	Caa	CCC
	Ca	CC
Extremely	C	C*
In Default	Ddd	DDD
	Dd	DD
	D	D

* Reserved for income bonds not paying interest.

If you do not feel up to struggling with the accounting records, the ratings given bonds by either *Moody's* or *S&P's* make a quite satisfactory substitute. They are widely used by both private and institutional investors at the present time.

Having assembled the five bits of essential information, then, you are now in a position to fill out a worksheet for bond purchase candidates to help you decide whether or not to buy.

BOND PURCHASE WORKSHEET

Name of Company: ______________________

(1) Current selling price ______________________

(2) Annual interest ______________________

(3) Years to maturity ______________________

(4) Maturity value ______________________

(5) Quality Rating ______________________
(*Moody's, S&P's,* or independent)

(6) Current yield ______________________
(2 divided by 1)

(7) Yield-to-maturity ______________________
(find in standard tables using 1, 2, 3 and 4)

(8) Appreciation
if held to maturity ______________________
(4 minus 1)

Using the results entered in lines 4, 5, 6, 7, and 8 of the Bond Purchase Worksheet, you are now in a position to decide whether you should actually buy the bond. In reaching a decision, check the following guidelines.

I	*Quality:* (line 5)	Buy only if entry here is A or better. In the 1970's, *do not* buy a bond that has less than an A rating.
II	*Yields:* (lines 6 & 7)	There are 3 guidelines: (a) Any time in the 1970's that a bond is available with an A or better rating and yields 8% or more, currently or to maturity, it is a *buy.* (b) If a bond rated A, or better, sells to yield 5% currently, or 5½% to maturity, or lower, *do not* buy in the 1970's. Corollary to (b): Any time in the 1970's that a bond you may be holding appreciates in price until its fixed interest payment provides a yield of 5% currently, or 5½% to maturity, take your profits by selling, freeing the cash, and putting your money to work earning you a higher current return. (c) If an A rated bond sells to yield between 5½% and less than 8% any time in the 1970's, check the current yields in other fixed-income investments and buy only if the *current yield* (not yield-to-maturity) appears favorable. Ignore yield-to-maturity; long-term yields in corporate bonds are not worth nailing down in this range.
III	*Appreciation:* (line 8)	If your marginal tax rate is 35% or higher, a higher number here will give you tax-sheltered income and is worth consideration in the decision to buy. At less than a 35% marginal tax rate, give little weight to this factor. Waiting for appreciation and its long-term capital gains tax benefits adds some risk, and this added risk is not worth taking unless the potential tax benefits are large—35% or higher.
IV	*How Long Must I Hold:* (line 4)	If you must hold five years or longer to realize the indicated yield-to-maturity and the yield-to-maturity is well above the current rate, then try to find a bond that will deliver the same yield-to-maturity in five years, or less. It pays to be flexible in the 1970's.

To summarize, follow these buying rules for bonds in the 1970's:

(1) Never buy a bond with a rating less than A. It never pays to trade quality for yield, especially in the 1970's.

(2) Limiting your purchases to A-rated bonds; in the 1970's quality bonds are always a buy at yields (currently or to maturity) of 8%, or better.

(3) Never take on the risk of a corporate bond, even an A-rated one, if it has a yield-to-maturity of less than 5½%. Series E bonds pay 5½% currently if held to maturity, offer much greater safety, and they cost nothing to buy.

(Series E bonds can be purchased without any charges. You can even purchase them through a payroll savings plan. Other bonds have charges, but these charges are generally less than those for purchasing other securities. Costs vary somewhat, but the average is around $2.50 for each $1,000 bought or sold. Bonds held to maturity do not have a selling fee.)

(4) If bond yields decline generally, you will have a profit if you are holding bonds bought when yields were higher. When the yields of bonds fall, their prices rise. To illustrate: assume that the XYZ corporation has an A-rated bond with 17 years left to maturity. XYZ's bond pays a $65 interest coupon and sells at about $928.50 to yield 7% currently. Let us further assume that the current yields on all other A-rated bonds with about 17 years left to maturity suddenly decline to 6% current yields. Then, the holder of an XYZ bond, bought at $928.50 when current yields were 7%, will now be able to sell his bond for $1,083 because other investors will now be willing to pay this much for the $65 coupon on the XYZ bond. This is so because $65 is 6% of $1,083 and 6% is what investors are now willing to accept as returns on other A-rated bonds of similar maturities. As a result, the holder of the XYZ bond will show a profit of $154.50 on his investment (the difference between the $928.50 purchase price and the $1,083 he can sell it for). He can take this profit by selling his bond.

At the present time, many high-quality bonds are selling at current yields of 8%, or better. If yields in general decline sometime later in the 1970's, holders of these bonds will have profits running in their portfolios of bonds, which they can nail down by selling. If you own bonds bought when interest rates were 8% or better, you should take your profits by selling if and when interest rates dip to 6%. At least until the late 1970's, bond yields are unlikely to get much below 6% (U.S. Government Series E bonds yield 5½% and Series H 6½% and better currently). At least, you can take your profits and reduce your risks by buying Series E or H bonds. At best, you can put your principal plus your profits from the sale of your bonds to work earning better yields. If bond yields slide in the 1970's, other investments, including common stocks, might have greater investment potentials.

(5) The only time you may get mixed signals in the case of bonds would be at a time in which corporate bonds sell to yield 6% to 7%, either currently or to maturity. Long-term, these yields are not particularly interesting; therefore, when bonds are selling in these yield ranges, you should consider only *current* yields. Whether you should buy bonds for current yields of 6% or 7% will depend largely on your opportunities elsewhere. If you cannot decide, then stay flexible by putting your funds into Series E or H bonds and waiting for clearer signals.

In addition to corporate bonds, you might also be interested in municipal bonds. As already noted, their interest payments are not subject to the Federal income tax. If you are interested in buying municipals, fill out the Bond Purchase Worksheet in this chapter. In the yield lines (6 and 7) however, also find the *corporate* yields that would be equivalent to the tax-exempt yields in municipals. The formula was outlined in Chapter 7. You will find, for instance, that an 8% taxable yield is equivalent to a 6% tax-sheltered yield in municipals, if you are in the 35% tax bracket.

Another special type of debt issue that might prove useful in the 1970's is Treasury bills. These are short-term obligations of the U.S. Treasury, maturing in three, six, nine, and twelve months. Their yields are variable, being closely related to conditions in the short-term money markets. They offer safe havens for investors with funds temporarily idle, awaiting better and more timely longer-run commitments. On occasion, when the yields are especially high, they are even attractive in themselves as income-investments. Of course, because of their short maturities, they have limits as assured income.

All of the rules in this chapter refer to straight bonds. They do not apply to convertible bonds (these types of bonds are discussed later in Chapter 16). In the quotation tables in your daily newspaper, convertible bonds are identified by a "cv" following the bond name.

In the next chapter, we will consider investments in raw land (land with improvements—real estate—will be discussed in Chapter 13). Unlike bonds, raw land pays no yields while held, its primary attraction being its appreciation potential over the years held.

CHAPTER 10

Raw Land—Does It Pay to Buy It?

In 1900, estimated land values in the United States were $32 billion. By 1960, total land was valued at approximately $300 billion, a tenfold gain in 60 years. Since 1960, land values have gained another $100 billion, an increase of about one-third, or a rise of about 12½ times since 1900.

Gains in individual areas have been even more spectacular. Between 1945 and 1970, prices of raw land in many parts of Long Island, New York, rose between 1,000–3,000%. Similar gains have been experienced in the same period in a number of areas of the country, including Atlanta, Boston, Charlotte, Cleveland, Dallas, Denver, Hartford, Los Angeles, Milwaukee, Orlando, Phoenix, San Francisco, and Seattle. Land in Vermont and New Hampshire, much of it selling at $50 and $100 an acre only ten years ago, is now commanding prices of several hundred dollars an acre.

Indeed, since the Pilgrims landed, one of the steadiest and more reliable sources of financial gain to American families has been the buying and selling of land. Even over the last decade, in many areas the prices of residential houses have appreciated sharply, with many existing homes selling for double what their owners paid for them only ten years earlier. Much of this increase did not result from the house, but reflected the increased price of building lots in these communities over the decade.

With these examples before them, both from the past and in the present, it is small wonder that many U.S. families have been seeking land investments in recent years. But a note of caution is in order.

While it is true that land values as a whole will undoubtedly continue to increase in the 1970's and beyond, it may not be true of individual plots of land. Despite the vast open areas available to them, 70% of the total U.S. population presently lives on only 1% of the land area. Most Americans live in or near urban centers, which reduces the acreage needed. True, there is expected to be some modest trend away from this intense concentration in the '70's, with many urban centers already experiencing a net loss of population. But even then, future projections call for 80% of the population to be living on only 1½% of the total land available.

So it is clear that while some land will become more valuable over the next decade and into the 1980's, it is also clear that not all of the land area in the U.S. will appreciate greatly, even if current trends hold. For the potential investor in raw land, the most important question is: Which land in the U.S. will appreciate in the 1970's, making it a timely purchase now? Since raw land normally provides no return whatsoever to its owner during the years in which it is held, the timing of the expected appreciation in its value becomes crucial in determining whether it pays as an investment.

For example, suppose that 100 acres of raw land becomes available at $100 an acre. It will require an investment of $10,000 now to purchase it. Mortgage money is difficult to find for raw land. Most mortgage lending institutions cannot, by law, lend money for the purchase of unimproved land that is not to be developed immediately. This leaves the buyer chiefly dependent for financing on other local financial institutions, such as banks, since lenders outside of the area are reluctant to put up money to finance property they cannot conveniently inspect. But even local lenders will be somewhat reluctant to finance something that is not producing income.

Let us suppose the buyer puts up $10,000 in cash, having withdrawn it from a savings bank that is paying him 5% a year interest. After he acquires the land, there will be taxes. Let us assume a modest $1 an acre or $100 a year.

Having bought the land, the buyer has lost $500 a year in bank interest and has to put up for taxes another $100 a year that could have been invested. At the end of ten years, he will have lost $6,288 in interest and paid $1,258 on the taxes, money that he could also have been putting away each year at 5%, making a total of $7,546.

If he cannot sell his land on favorable terms at the end of the first ten years, he can go on holding. But the costs of holding continue to rise. At the end of twenty years he will have lost $16,532 interest on his original $10,000 invested in the land, and if he had invested the $100 annual taxes at 5%, he would have an additional $3,307, for a total of $19,839. This means that even if his land doubles in value—if it takes twenty years—he could have done just about as well banking the money and never buying the land.

Even if his land had doubled in value by the end of the first ten years, he would have made only about $2,500 more out of the land than he would have made by leaving the $10,000 in the savings bank and investing the $100 taxes each year. And this example assumes that there are no selling commissions on either end, that there were no special assessments on the land while he held it, and that he had to make no improvements of the land to enhance its sale value. Any one of these things would have reduced his $2,500 net gain from buying the land, assuming a sale at the end of ten years. It would have resulted in *no net advantages* over the savings bank if he had to hold for twenty years.

Quite clearly, increasing the length of the holding period does not improve this investment. If he had to hold for thirty years, he would have had to pay $3,000 in taxes, let alone the interest, and lost $33,210 in interest on the $10,000 sunk into the land. There is such a thing as being land poor.

Before you consider buying raw land, you should work out some of this arithmetic, paying close attention to the workout time required to justify a current investment. Here is a worksheet that can be adapted to your own situation:

RAW LAND PURCHASE WORKSHEET

Land Plot Identification ____________________

(1) Current price ____________________

(2) Annual return on
self-supplied funds ____________________
(what they are earning, what they could earn)

(3) Estimated annual taxes ____________________

(4) *Ten-year cost of holding*
(a) 10-year earnings on
funds self-supplied (if
they were invested) ____________________
(b) Taxes (invested
at the same rate) ____________________
(c) Financing costs
(if any) ____________________
Total cost of holding
(a + b + c) ____________________

(5) *20-year cost of holding*
(a) 20-year earnings on

funds self-supplied (if they were invested) ______

(b) 20-year taxes (invested at same rate) ______

(c) Financing costs (if any) ______

Total cost of holding (a + b + c) ______

Filling in the lines of this worksheet will help you focus on the potentials that you must see in a piece of raw land if it is to be a good investment and highlights the importance of the time-span involved in a good raw land investment.

You should be able to classify all of the potential parcels of raw land that you might consider buying under one of the following three headings:

(1) Raw Land—Future Uses Unknown
(2) Raw Land—Future Uses Known, with Some Probability
(3) Raw Land—Future Uses Known, and You Know How to Speed Up the Timetable

Type 3 raw land investments are in many respects the most desirable, having a pay-out time that is capable of being realized within a limited span. However, to keep this pay-out time on schedule, a Type 3 situation may take more of the investor's time and cash funds than he is realistically able to contribute. In some instances, it may require that he be able to become the actual developer of the raw land, able to contribute the time and the additional funds to activate this pay-out. In other cases, it may mean that the purchaser of the raw land creates a selling brochure, which may cost $1,000 or so first to produce and then to locate a mailing list of live prospects to receive it. In short, at the time of purchase—or better still at the time he takes an option to buy—the enterprising purchaser of raw land should have in mind several good potential uses of the land, be able and willing to publicize these uses, and possibly even be willing to undertake some of them himself in order to keep the time-span of his investment within acceptable profit limits.

If a buyer of raw land is either unwilling or unable to become an enterprising purchaser in a Type 3 situation, he should at least attempt to find a Type 2 situation, which already has several fairly well-known potential uses but has as yet failed to attract a promoter. Obviously, he will have to pay more for this parcel of raw land than he would for a Type 3 situation, but at least he has a fighting chance of realizing his appreciation before the long-term costs of carrying the investment begin to eat deeply into his profit potential. A Type 2 investor in raw land can be wrong. It is well known that land use patterns depend on a host of factors, such as business conditions in the area, population growth and—not the least—the vagaries of local politics and politicians. But at least a Type 2 investor has a chance—70–40, or 50–50.

In any case, a Type 2 investor is almost always better off than a Type 1 investor, who has no ideas himself about possible future uses of the land and as far as he can determine, neither does anyone else. While he may be able to get his raw land at a cheaper price than either a Type 2 or a Type 3 investor, his waiting period may easily erase any initial gain the lower cost may give him. He is the real land speculator, while Type 3 is an enterprising investor and Type 2 is an investor who is convinced that the wait for one of the known potential uses to materialize is worth his time and money. Put another way: if you are of the opinion that all investment is a type of "speculation," then Type 2 and Type 3 purchases are sensible speculations, while Type 1 is likely to be a time-waster.

Some investors prefer to invest or speculate in improved land, reasoning that they get the land plus an income-producing property to help pay for the costs of waiting. While it is true that land under existing structures continues to appreciate generally along with land values, improved land has already taken its first step up in its escalation from raw land values. Although future resales may reflect this higher evaluation, some of the profit margin between raw and developed land prices will already have been skimmed off. For a discussion of the potentials of investing in land *plus* improvement, see Chapter 13.

While some investors feel that raw land in remote areas has little appeal, they are nevertheless attracted to owning something that, like land, is real, tangible, and has a value that is capable of appreciation after a reasonable waiting period. Some of these types of real asset holdings are reviewed next, in Chapter 11.

CHAPTER 11

Real Assets—The Hedge Value of Gemstones, Antiques, and Art Objects: Real or Mythical?

If you would like to be a Renaissance man (and who wouldn't in these dull days of specialization), you might want to surround yourself in your home with a group of tasteful and select objects that, while they earn you nothing, do enrich your idle moments, add to your status and might someday deliver a handsome capital gain. That's the scenario—here's the real story.

Real assets (gemstones, antiques, art objects), like raw land, generally earn no income while they are held. But unlike raw land, they have an additional handicap—you can't just let them lie around unattended. One of their features is high value in a relatively small space, which means that they are easy to steal. Insurance can take care of that but it does cost something. Also, most of these assets require some special type of storage, or display, which again means money.

Most of these real assets unfortunately are traded on very special markets. Usually you have to buy at retail, but if you are in a hurry to sell, you have to accept wholesale prices, since the only ready buyer is usually a dealer. Some can be sold at auctions, but this takes time.

But perhaps the greatest drawback of all is the fact that a timely and potentially profitable purchase of most of these assets requires considerable expert knowledge—not only an ability to spot a fake, but also a sixth sense that tells you what these assets will be worth in a year or a decade from now. If experts disagree (and they do about most of these assets), can an amateur succeed?

Perhaps the best way to gain insight into some of the problems connected with investing in real assets is to review briefly some of the opportunities in this area:

Gemstones: Avoid cut gems in settings. Fashions in both settings and cuts change. Uncut gems have the best appreciation potential, but, of course, they are less fun to own.

Coin Collections: Mint sets bought from the issuer, *not* the dealer, require the least specialized knowledge and do about as well as an average coin collection on the market.

Stamp Collections: Unused stamps bought from the issuer, *not* the dealer, are preferred. Try US, UK, UN, Canada, and Israeli singles, blocks, and sheets.

Book and Manuscript Collections: Specialize in a period, or a topic. Collections can often be sold on better terms than individual items—you are being paid for assembling the collection as well as for the individual items.

Fads in Collections: Old comic books, barbed wire—people can and do collect anything. Whether anyone will pay you for a specialized collection is another matter.

Antiques: Furniture, snuff boxes, bric-a-brac. Trends shift rapidly here, from period to period. Obviously, the biggest potentials come from being ahead of the trends. Often a long shot.

Art: This has done very well in recent years. But before you plunge in, ask yourself the following questions: Where are those dull canvases you were told were Great Art when you were a child? Who owns them now, and what would they bring on the open market today?

Cattle, Forests, and Scotch Whiskey in Vats: These have been popular as tax-shelters among the higher-tax bracket set in recent years. You buy the cattle, trees, or raw whiskey, pay the carrying charges over the years (which are tax deductions when paid), and sell your asset—when it fattens, grows into a mighty oak, or mellows—for a capital gain, which shelters the income from Federal taxes. However, although you do not have to know anything about cows, trees, or whiskey to play, you *do* have to know the cattleman, forester, or vintner with whom you are dealing, since you and he will be involved in a relationship for a number of years. You can't win unless he is both reasonably honest and is present at pay-off time.

This is a representative, not exhaustive, list of real assets that you might consider acquiring. We might add race horses, but they are notoriously bad investments. In fact, almost all of these real assets can be disastrous investments for those without the time or the inclination to acquire specialized knowledge. For those who wish to dabble in this area, then coin and stamp collections—if you stick with mint issues bought only from the issuer, *never* dealers—can do about as well for you as any of the less expensive items. For those who desire a larger commitment, gemstones can absorb large blocks of cash, are easy to store, and have a good track record. If you are worried about the possibility of synthetic gemstones, remember that "real" pearls are still treasured despite the spread of cultured pearls. Coins, stamps, and gemstones all have the added advantage of providing suitable collateral for loans while they are being held, which can help you reduce somewhat the net costs of waiting for the expected appreciations.

Most of these real assets offer a good hedge against inflation, which will make them useful through most of the 1970's. Most of them have international markets and are good hedges against possible future dollar devaluations in the 1970's. Only in deflationary periods or depressions do these real assets pose a problem. When Wall Street takes a plunge, Tiffany feels the downdraft. So, if you do decide to buy into real assets as good hedges against inflation and devaluation, make limited commitments so you will not be locked in during deflationary times (unless, of course, you see an extremely short workout time for your appreciation). Before making a commitment, fill in the following worksheet:

REAL ASSET PURCHASE WORKSHEET

Type of Asset ________________

(1) Current Purchase Price ________________

(2) Annual Return on Self-Supplied Funds ________________
(what they are earning, what they could earn)

(3) Estimated Annual Costs of Insurance, Storage, etc. ________________

(4) Amount that Could Be Borrowed, Using This Asset as Collateral ________________

(5) Cost of This Type of Borrowing ________________

(6) Estimated Appreciation ____________
(7) Tax-Shelter, If Any, on
Capital Gains ____________
(8) Net Appreciation
(after taxes) ____________
(9) Estimated Workout Time ____________
(10) Annual Average Net ____________
(8 divided by 9)

Having completed the Real Asset Purchase Worksheet, make the following assessments:

(a) Compare line 10 with lines 2 and 3. If line 10 exceeds lines 2 and 3 by a wide margin, you can then make the following further comparison.
(b) Compare line 10 with the last lines on other Real Asset Purchase Worksheets. Consider only the highest last line.
(c) Compare the best last lines among real assets with the annual gains you can make in other areas, particularly bonds (see worksheet in Chapter 9) and raw land (in Chapter 10). The basis for this comparison is that bonds (if you limit your purchases to A rated bonds), raw land, and real assets have one characteristic in common: namely, all of these are sheltered from business risk—A rated bonds because of their quality, raw land, and real assets because they are not income-producing property.

But there is a further point to be made here. Since you are taking less risk, all three may provide you with lower yields. Now, if the yields available in these low-risk investments appear unsatisfactory to you at a given moment, then you will have to be willing to trade security for yield, taking on a little more risk to achieve the desired higher yield.

In Part IV, we will review a number of income-producing assets whose income is exposed to the hazards of business risk, but whose yields are often better than can be obtained from the low-risk investments we have just covered.

Part IV

HOW TO INSURE YOUR "EDGE"—REDUCING THE RISKS WHILE INCREASING THE RETURNS

CHAPTER 12

Timing—When to Buy (and How) and When to Sell

While you wait for a pot to boil, the time that counts is elapsed time; but once the pot is at the boil, *timing* (putting in the ingredients in proper sequence) is what matters. When you buy bonds, raw land, and real assets, the waiting time until you can gather in your earnings is what counts; but, when you buy income-producing assets, you will do better if you buy them just before a big surge in earnings. Thus, *timing* becomes more important than what is bought. This is what a stock market trader means when he says: "Don't tell me what to buy; just tell me when to buy it."

Ben ("Sell 'Em Short Ben") Smith became a Wall Street legend by "shorting" the market in 1929. There were doubtlessly a few passengers who missed the sailing of the Titanic, but consider those who made it to the sailing on time. Most of us do not have to be convinced that timing is important in almost any undertaking. But there are problems, especially in the timing of the purchase of income-producing assets. The economic clock has no hands, only hundreds of little gauges, all of them giving different readings.

There are those who devote their working hours almost exclusively to reading the gauges on the economic clock. Eventually they select a few gauges that seem to be keeping economic time most accurately—and then announce to the world what time it is on stock markets, commodity markets, and all of the markets for the outputs of industry. Of course, it usually turns out that they had been watching the wrong gauges, because the alarm bell goes off well ahead of schedule, waking everyone from dreams of riches or nightmares of hard times—depending on the economic diet they have been fed recently—well before anyone is ready to cope with a new day.

This inability of economic gauge-watchers, stock market gauge-watchers and other assorted forecasters to tell investment time with any degree of precision has led some investors to search for ways to ignore timing. The simplest, and one of the best, of all of the formulas to beat timing is "dollar cost averaging." An investor, feeling that he (or she), can never know exactly when the right buying time arrives, uses a dollar cost averaging formula to accumulate a desired asset and simply decides to spend a *constant dollar amount* periodically on the asset.

Let's say he decides to spend $1,000 every year on an asset. In a year in which prices of this asset decline, with his fixed $1,000 he automatically buys more. Uncertain about where prices will go, he then spends nothing more on this but waits until the next year. When it arrives, if prices turn out to be even lower, his $1,000 automatically buys more. On the other hand, if prices rise instead, he still spends his fixed $1,000, without asking whether it is a good or a bad time to buy, but of course buys *less.* If in the third year after he put this plan into operation, prices really skyrocket, he will automatically accumulate fewer of these assets than he did in the first two years of the program. The point is, that over a number of years of accumulation, by spending a fixed $1,000 each year he will have automatically accumulated his asset at the lowest *average* cost possible.

What happens if prices are high in the year the dollar cost averaging program is started and that while prices fluctuate during the following years of accumulation, they never reach the former high? Does dollar cost averaging work here? Let us put dollar cost averaging to a severe test—by using the stock market and assuming that you had bought at the high in 1929.

Just how a dollar cost averaging program would have worked out during the sickening slide of 1929 and the early 1930's is illustrated in the table that follows. In this case, it is assumed that $1,000 is invested at the *absolute high* in each year between 1929 and 1973. By assuming purchases at the highs, any chance of tricks of the calendar—an especially favorable buying point in one specific month—is ruled out.

Despite this obvious handicap of always buying at the top, such a dollar averaging portfolio initiated in 1929 would have started to show a profit as early as 1935. At the 1937 high on the market, which was still well below the

1929 high, such a program would have shown a profit of $2,266 over its $9,000 cost to that point, or an appreciation of 25.1%.

The recession of 1937 quickly melted most of these profits, but the program still managed to just about break even until 1940, when war clouds created large market uncertainties. However, by 1944 the portfolio was again moving into the profit column. It might be noted that at its high in 1944, the Dow-Jones industrial average was still 229 points, or about 60% below its 1929 high.

With the end of World War II, the dollar averaging program began to move well ahead of costs. By 1954, when after twenty-five years the Dow-Jones industrials again equaled their 1929 high, this dollar averaging portfolio had a market value of $60,242, as compared with a cost of $26,000.

The return of the Dow to its 1929 high might have been a logical point to have closed out this dollar-averaging program. In that case, the investor would have realized an appreciation of 131.7%, or an average return of about 5% per year during the 26 years the program was in operation. While this may seem somewhat modest, it must be recalled that these 26 years included the greatest depression ever known, the largest scale war ever waged, and the biggest peacetime intervention in history in Korea—events unlikely to steady investors' nerves and build confidence.

Of course, if a dollar-averaging program had been initiated in 1954, it would have performed admirably. The Dow-Jones industrials rose by about 164%, between 1954 and 1973. But even if the dollar-averaging program initiated in 1929 had been continued, it would have brought even more impressive results, the market value of the portfolio going from $60,242 in 1954 to $185,650, a gain of over 200%. In 1973, this portfolio would have cost $45,000 (ignoring commission costs) to accumulate. In its 45 years of operation, a total appreciation of 313% would have been realized for an annual average of 7%.

You might notice that the dollar averaging plan illustrated in the table has been having difficulty making upward progress in terms of its total market value since 1966. Only three times, in 1968 and again in 1972 and 1973, was it ever higher than in 1966. And in the 1969–70 slide, the total value was actually lower than it had been in 1964, despite the fact that 5.35 composite "shares" had been added to the portfolio from 1965 through 1971. In the twelve-month period between early 1973 and early 1974, the market suffered a sharp setback, taking the Dow-Jones industrial average down over 200 points from the all-time high established in early 1973 of 1,067.20. As a result, the 173.96 "shares" of the 30 Dow-Jones stocks that were assumed to have been accumulated by the end of 1973 in the table and

YEAR	AMOUNT INVESTED	PRICE* (COST PER UNIT)	NUMBER OF UNITS BOUGHT	TOTAL NUMBER BOUGHT	TOTAL COST**	TOTAL MARKET VALUE
1929	$1,000	$ 381.17***	2.62	2.62	$ 1,000	$ 1,000
1930	1,000	294.07	3.40	6.02	2,000	1,770
1931	1,000	194.36	5.15	11.17	3,000	2,171
1932	1,000	88.78	11.26	22.43	4,000	1,991
1933	1,000	108.67	9.20	31.63	5,000	3,437
1934	1,000	110.74	9.03	40.66	6,000	4,503
1935	1,000	148.44	6.74	47.40	7,000	7,036†
1936	1,000	184.90	5.41	52.81	8,000	9,765
1937	1,000	194.40	5.14	57.95	9,000	11,266
1938	1,000	158.41	6.31	64.26	10,000	10,179
1939	1,000	155.92	6.41	70.67	11,000	11,019
1940	1,000	152.80	6.54	77.21	12,000	11,798
1941	1,000	133.59	7.49	84.70	13,000	11,315
1942	1,000	119.71	8.35	93.05	14,000	11,139
1943	1,000	145.82	6.86	99.91	15,000	14,569
1944	1,000	152.53	6.56	106.47	16,000	16,240
1945	1,000	195.82	5.11	111.58	17,000	21,850
1946	1,000	212.50	4.71	116.29	18,000	24,712
1947	1,000	186.85	5.35	121.64	19,000	22,728
1948	1,000	193.16	5.18	126.82	20,000	24,497
1949	1,000	200.52	4.99	131.81	21,000	26,431
1950	1,000	235.47	4.25	136.06	22,000	32,038†
1951	1,000	276.37	3.62	139.68	23,000	38,603
1952	1,000	292.00	3.42	143.10	24,000	41,785
1953	1,000	293.79‡	3.40	146.50	25,000	43,040
1954	1,000	404.39‡	2.47	148.97	26,000	60,242
1955	1,000	488.40	2.05	151.02	27,000	73,758
1956	1,000	521.05	1.92	152.94	28,000	79,689
1957	1,000	520.77	1.92	154.86	29,000	80,646
1958	1,000	583.65	1.71	156.57	30,000	91,382
1959	1,000	679.36	1.47	158.04	31,000	107,366
1960	1,000	685.47	1.46	159.50	32,000	109,332
1961	1,000	734.91	1.36	160.86	33,000	118,700
1962	1,000	726.01	1.38	162.24	34,000	117,788
1963	1,000	767.21	1.30	163.54	35,000	125,470
1964	1,000	891.71	1.12	164.66	36,000	146,829
1965	1,000	969.26	1.03	165.69	37,000	160,597
1966	1,000	995.15	1.01	166.70	38,000	165,892
1967	1,000	943.08	1.06	167.76	39,000	158,101

carried over into 1974 would have been worth only about $147,850 at an average price of 850 for the 30 Dow industrials in the early months of 1974. This would have been a portfolio value just about equal to that in 1970 and 1964, despite the fact that there were more "shares" of the 30 Dow industrials in the portfolio in 1974 than in either of these earlier years, 2.96 units more than in 1970 and 9.30 units more than in 1964. Also, at 850, the portfolio was worth $37,800 less than at its peak in early 1973, or a decline of slightly over 20%. We will have to take a hard look at the sluggishness of the stock market over the past eight years when we discuss the stock investment opportunities in the 1970's and beyond, in Chapter 14.

If you feel that you have neither the time nor the ability to pinpoint correct buying (and selling) timing, then you may use dollar cost averaging—a fixed sum each quarter or year—to accumulate any of the assets discussed in this book during the 1970's. Dollar cost averaging will also fit with the way your income is earned if most of your earnings result from wages, salaries, or fees that come to you on a fairly regular basis. Using the 10% rule (see Chapter 8), you will be freeing cash for investment on a fairly regular schedule. This can become your fixed amount for regular, periodic investment under dollar cost averaging.

If you feel you can devote the time and effort needed to pinpoint "good" and "bad" times to buy and sell, then you can adapt dollar cost averaging simply by reducing the fixed sum you invest when your signals say that it is a "bad" time to invest. Funds saved from "bad" buying times can be used to *increase* the sum invested when your signals flash green. This would, of course, further reduce the amounts you accumulate at unfavorable buying

YEAR	AMOUNT INVESTED	PRICE* (COST PER UNIT)	NUMBER OF UNITS BOUGHT	TOTAL NUMBER BOUGHT	TOTAL COST**	TOTAL MARKET VALUE
1968	1,000	985.21	1.02	168.78	40,000	166,284
1969	1,000	965.85	1.03	169.81	41,000	164,610
1970	1,000	842.00	1.19	171.00	42,000	143,982
1971	1,000	950.82	1.05	172.05	43,000	163,589
1972	1,000	1,036.27	0.97	173.02	44,000	179,295
1973	1,000	1,067.20	0.94	173.96	45,000	185,650

* Annual High
** Ignoring Commisions
*** Dow-Jones high in 1929
† First year since 1929 in which dollar-averaging program in Dow-Jones broke even.
‡ Between 1953 and 1954 the Dow-Jones average returned to its 1929 highs (381.70) for the first time in 25 years.

points and greatly increase the amounts you accumulate at favorable points. But if you do attempt to adjust your fixed dollar investment sum by your own subjective evaluations of "good" and "bad" times to buy, proceed with caution until you have proven out your timing method.

One additional point should be made: whether you use the standard or adjusted dollar cost averaging program, *never fail* to make your scheduled investment when things look bleak. If you fail to invest when prices are lower, even though you feel they might go lower still (and they may), you will upset the long-term effectiveness of any dollar cost averaging program by failing to take advantage of lower prices when they are available. If prices do go lower, you will be buying more in the next round of accumulation. If prices go higher, you will have a profit. Very often, market traders who attempt to get the absolute bottom price miss the market, and those who try to squeeze the last dollar out at the top often see their profits slide away. Using dollar cost averaging, you may never buy at the bottom, but you will accumulate a profitable position if you stick with it.

Having established a plan for timing your purchases of income-producing assets, all you need is candidates for purchase. In Chapter 13, we will take a brief look at one such candidate, income-earning property—real estate.

CHAPTER 13

Real Estate—It Is Real, but Can You Build an Estate with It?

Landlords, slum and otherwise, are held in low repute by many. This fact alone may give you pause when you consider becoming a landlord yourself.

One reason many property owners make poor landlords is that the game they are playing is called *resale.* Here's how this game is played: put up as little of your own money as you can, get the maximum mortgage, hope that the rents of your tenants carry the deal and leave something over to reward you while you are waiting to sell for a capital gain.

There are two reasons why you can play this game with real estate—land plus improvements—and not with raw land:

(1) Existing improvements on land that produce an income enable you to get a mortgage on real estate more easily than you can with raw land by itself.

(2) You can depreciate this improvement on land for tax purposes; raw land cannot be depreciated. Further, interest on your mortgage and maintenance expenses are tax deductible. (Also, as in the case of raw land, capital gains from resale are tax-sheltered.)

Thus, the availability of financing and the tax angles both favor real estate over raw land. But, as is only fair, there are more headaches when you hold real estate than when you hold raw land.

There's wear and tear you can't just write off—smudged hallway walls, broken doors, etc., which must be repaired as part of operating expenses. These costs are greater with residential property as compared with office buildings and commercial.

Tenants can decline to renew their leases; so you had better have a built-in assumption of at least a 10% vacancy rate.

Real estate has to be managed, rents collected, heat maintained. If you do not wish to do this yourself, there are added expenses.

And in the 1970's, there are uncertainties about formal or informal rent "regulations," fuel and maintenance cost rises, possible tenant rent strikes as all prices inflate, and all of the other inflation-related problems connected with owning and operating rental property. Your rent rolls should be about 10% of the total purchase price of your real estate, including any renovation spending necessary. If the rent income, allowing a 10% vacancy rate, is less than 10% of total outlays to acquire the building, you probably will not be able to survive until resale time. At a minimum, interest on the mortgage, taxes, and upkeep have to come out of the rent rolls.

The following worksheet will help keep these factors in perspective—though in this case, as we shall see, it basically provides only a starting point.

REAL ESTATE PURCHASE WORKSHEET

Property Name ______________________
(1) Purchase Price ______________________
(2) Renovations, if any ______________________
(3) Funds Self-Supplied ______________________
(4) Mortgage Available ______________________
(5) Annual Mortgage Costs ______________________
(6) Annual Property Taxes ______________________
(7) Annual Upkeep Costs ______________________
(8) Annual Rents ______________________
(allowing 10% vacancy rate)
(9) Cash Flow (8 minus 5+6+7) ______________________
(10) Annual Earnings ______________________
(9 minus depreciation on 1 & 2, with 1 depreciated over 15–20 years and 2 depreciated over 5 years)

(11) Expected Sale Price ______________________________
(12) Expected Number of Years to Resale ______________________

With the data in the Real Estate Purchase Worksheet, you should be able to reach a preliminary decision as to whether a piece of real estate is worth closer inspection. Whatever the worksheet may show, you will want to make an extensive physical investigation before taking an option to buy. You will want to know such things as the rents in adjacent buildings, zoning laws as applied to the block in which the property is located, something about the possible future of the neighborhood, etc. But some attention to the figures on your worksheet will let you know whether it pays to find these things out about a specific piece of property.

For instance, if line 8 on the worksheet is not at least 10% of lines 1 plus 2, you should consider other purchases. If, for whatever reason, line 4 (the mortgage available) is not at least 90% of lines 1 plus 2, you may also want to reconsider, since line 3 (self-supplied funds) will be more than 10% of initial outlays required (lines 1 plus 2). Line 12—the number of years before expected resale—must be examined in light of lines 5, 6, and 7, your total annual expenses of waiting. If these expenses are large, then line 12 must be no more than 5 years if you are to realize full capital gains benefits from line 11 (resale price) minus lines 1 plus 2 (your initial outlays). If expenses of holding are high, you will have paid too high a price for these capital gains.

So far we have considered only general factors connected with the purchase, holding and eventual sale of real estate. What are the prospects for the 1970's? Of course, local conditions will be of paramount importance; but the following general observations may be made about real estate values in the 1970's, nationwide:

Middle-income and luxury residential rental property should continue to make a satisfactory investment in the 1970's. Residential rental property in declining or slum neighborhoods was becoming less attractive almost year-by-year in the 1960's, and there appears little reason to expect a reverse trend here in the 1970's, especially if either continued regulations or general price inflation makes it difficult to get "satisfactory" increases in rentals. If you are interested in acquiring residential real estate, limit yourself to apartment buildings or multiple-family units in good neighborhoods that are holding their own in the 1970's.

Many investors prefer office buildings or commercial property to residential holdings—there are generally fewer day-to-day headaches with business tenants. However, in the early 1970's investments here may prove untimely, especially in office buildings. Boston, Dallas, Los Angeles, New York, and Pittsburgh are all already reporting higher vacancy rates in office space, even before new, large office buildings in many of these cities are completed and placed on the market. Many office space brokers said that 1972 was one of the toughest years for renting in some time and in many localities new buildings reaching completion kept things tight in 1973. Many feel that it will take two or three years to work down the present glut of unrented office space in many cities. Do not consider new purchases here until the outcome is better known.

With the wheat deals with Russia and the growing world demand for corn, wheat, and soybeans, some investors are considering investments in farm land that can be rented or leased to operators. Absentee landowners in profitable farm country, like the corn and soybean acreage in Illinois, realize about $25 an acre for rented farm land. With the average farm size about 400 acres, this means an annual income of $10,000. However, the cost of an *average* 400-acre farm is around $87,500 and in Illinois is closer to $125,000. So this means a return of only about 8–11% without allowing for taxes and the expenses of carrying the investment. If you are willing to operate your 400-acre farm instead of renting it, you can realize some $20,000 to $24,000; but the *minimum* investment for a 400-acre farm *plus* operating equipment is $200,000.

There is another factor affecting all types of real estate in the 1970's, all the way from single-family homes to giant office buildings, and that is the cost and availability of mortgage money. High costs and the inability to get to mortgage loans may keep a lot of potential buyers for all types of real estate off the market in the 1970's. This will make it all the harder for present owners of real estate properties to complete sales and actually realize the sale prices they think their properties should command.

In general, prospects in real estate do not appear especially promising for the early 1970's. The second half of the decade may bring a recovery, but unless you feel that you have found an unusual property, reflecting special local conditions, real estate appears to be a wait-and-see situation until at least the second half of the 1970's.

If you are still interested in real estate and property development, you might consider common stocks in that area—and guide your buying by the rules for common stock trading in the 1970's developed in the next chapter.

CHAPTER 14

Common Stocks— Gamble or Investment?

For 25 cents, you can take a chance on a Las Vegas one-armed bandit; for 50 cents to $1, in many states, you can buy a lottery ticket; $2 puts you on a horse. But to take a position in a 100-share, round lot of a $40 stock, you have to put up $4,000 and pay out around $100 in commissions and taxes to both buy and sell and thus realize your winnings, if any.

While you may or may not get back your $4,000, this $100 in commissions and taxes is a cost for "playing" in the market. So if you want to gamble, Wall Street is no place to do it, since it is one of the most expensive places around to place bets.

What should you be looking for if you should decide to buy and hold common stocks? Of course, there are only two ways a share of common stock can ever reward its holder:

(1) It can pay cash dividends.
(2) It can go up in price on the market, enabling the holder to sell it for more than he paid for it.

Which should you seek—cash dividends or market appreciation? In part, your answer might be affected by your tax bracket. Cash dividends are counted as regular income for purposes of the income tax and are taxed at your maximum rate (with the exception of the first $100 or the first $200 in a joint return, as explained in Chapter 7). However, if you make a profit on selling your stock, this profit is called a capital gain, and a *long-term* capital gain—the stock must be held for six months or longer—is taxed in most instances at a more favorable rate than you would pay at your marginal tax rate on regular income. As a result of the more favored tax treatment of long-term capital gains, some investors prefer capital gains to cash dividends, even though they have to wait longer to obtain the tax-sheltered capital gains. *Short-term* capital gains (or losses) result when the sale of a share of common stock takes place in less than six months after purchase; in this case, there is no tax-shelter.

While tax considerations cannot be ignored in your planning of stock purchases and sales, they are obviously less important than whether or not you will actually realize a cash dividend or a profit from a sale. Tax considerations aside, which should have the highest priority for you—cash dividends or the possibility of appreciation in the selling price of the stock? This is related to a second question: which is it more profitable to buy, stocks or bonds?

Much, of course, will depend on your family's present needs. If your family happens to be living through a period of especially high current spending—you are furnishing a house, a child is going away to college, you want to take that trip to Europe—then high cash dividends of course would be a welcome supplement to your regular income.

However, if extra current income for spending now is your *primary* objective, common stocks, bought and held chiefly for cash dividends that they are paying out, are a poor way to attempt to get it. In early 1974, for instance, high-grade stocks were selling to yield only about a 4¼% return, while high-grade bonds were yielding just under 8%. You could have earned more in a savings account—between 4½% and 5%—than you could have in an "average" high-grade common stock. Nor has this spread between bond and stock yields been a recent development—bonds have been paying higher yields than common stocks in every year since the late 1950's.

It may appear odd to you that bonds yield more than common stocks, since you are taking a greater risk when you buy a share of common stock than when you buy a bond. But while it is true that stocks are exposed to greater risks because of fluctuating business conditions, bonds held long-term are exposed to another sort of risk—the erosion through inflation of the buying power of the money invested. Over time at least, common stocks tend to rise in price, offering some offset to the risks of declining purchasing power from inflation.

For instance, in early 1959, the index of the thirty Dow industrial stocks had a reading of around 590. By early 1974, they were trading just around 850. Over the 15 years, this is an increase of about 44%, or an average annual gain of 2.9%. Over these 15 years, the 30 Dow industrials were yielding an average of about 3.6%, although yields fluctuated. So, in these years, by investing in these high-grade common stocks you would have experienced an average return of 6.5% each year—3.6% from the cash dividends and 2.9% from the average appreciation. This 6.5% *joint* yield from common stock was somewhat better than the 5.2% average yield available in high-grade bonds in these years.

Admittedly, the over 200 point slide in the Dow-Jones industrial average between early 1973 and early 1974 accounts for much of this rather poor showing in the results of buying and holding a representative portfolio of high-grade stocks over the 15 years since 1959. If the Dow were to recover its early 1973 all-time high of 1,067 sometime later in 1974 or by early 1975, the total appreciation would then be a more encouraging 81% since early 1959. This would be an average annual appreciation of about 5.1%. Put this together with the 3.6% average annual cash dividend yield of the Dow industrials and the *joint* yield is 8.7%, as compared with the 5.2% average current yields from a portfolio of high-grade bonds held since 1959.

It is interesting to note that when the yields available on high-grade bonds broke through 8%, as in 1970, common stocks were notably less popular, selling down sharply in price, and in early 1974, as high-grade yields rose toward 8%, common stocks hesitated. This would suggest 8% is a sort of investment threshold: at below 8% for high-grade bonds, investors are more willing to consider common stocks as long-term investments, but when yields of 8% or better are available on high-grade bonds, investors appear less willing to risk earning 8% or better in common stocks in favorable market periods, especially when it is evident that setbacks as experienced between early 1973 and early 1974 can cut back their long-term gains to unsatisfactory 6.5% rates, as was the case in early 1974. Apparently most investors, on their own, have concluded what computer studies of long-term market trends have confirmed—those investors who buy and hold *long enough* realize an annual *average* return of between 8–9% on their stock portfolios. Since this indicated 8–9% rate of return is an average there will be periods in which they may do better, but there are also stretches when they will do worse.

In recent years, while high-grade common stocks were yielding 3–4%, there was also a scattering of stocks yielding 8%, 10%, even 15% and higher. But when exceptionally high yields are available in common stocks, there is usually a reason—and this reason is usually not that the company is displaying superior performance.

In some cases, like mining stocks and real estate investment companies, the higher yields reflect pay-outs of depletion and depreciation allowances to the stockholders. Therefore they are unlikely to be of long duration—when the assets that are being depleted or depreciated are exhausted, the cash dividend will shrink to a lower level.

In other cases, higher cash dividends are being paid out of the fat of earlier years. As a result, the stock price has drifted down as the company's earnings are declining, and in some cases, even hitting deficits. Sooner or later, unless there is a sharp reversal in a company's prospects, these cash dividends will have to be cut.

So it is evident that if you are looking for *safe* yields, common stocks offer few, if any, real opportunities. All things considered, if high current yields are your primary objective, you will do better in bonds (see Chapter 9).

However, you may wish to seek some income from common stocks, realizing that, if you are to do as well as you can in bonds, you must invest in *Income Plus* situations. That is, the stock of companies that have paid cash dividends regularly for some time and, in addition, have been expanding their sales and profits at a sufficient rate to keep the common price rising annually somewhere in a 3% to 5% range. Such companies would provide you with some *dependable* current income and at the same time, through their rising stock prices, provide you with some offset to inflation.

However, you should understand quite well the limits of common stocks as inflation hedges. Over *long periods of time,* stock prices, on average, tend to move up as fast as the *average* rate of inflation, over a number of years. But, in short periods, stock prices may even decline while general prices increase, as the table below illustrates:

Annual Average Changes

YEARS	PRICE CHANGES (PRICES IN GNP)	DOW-JONES INDUSTRIAL STOCK PRICES
1958–1965 (7 year period)	+1.6%	+10.5%
1966–1973 (8 year period)	+4.8	−4.1
1958–1973 (total 15 years)	+2.6	+2.7

While it is evident in the table above that common stocks failed to provide a hedge against inflation in the years 1966–1973, it is also true that over the entire span of years, 1958 to 1973, the price appreciation in common stocks just about offset the 2.6% annual average increase in prices.

Even though the price appreciation in the Dow-Jones industrials did little more than keep their holders even with the inflation over the last 15 years, these stocks did provide an additional reward to their holders in these years by providing an annual average cash dividend yield of around 3.5%. As a result, *over the long haul*—15 years in this case—the common stocks in Dow average provided income *plus* an offset to inflation for their holders.

If you are interested in Income Plus stocks that offer you current dependable income plus a *long-term* offset to inflation, you might consider shopping among stocks with long-term records as cash dividend payers. A selected (not exhaustive) list of dependable long-term dividend payers is provided in the tables on pages 100 to 105.

Not all of the stocks listed in these tables will, of course, do equally well in a given year, or even over the 1970's as a whole and beyond. They have been dependable cash dividend payers *in the past,* but you are interested in the cash dividends they *will be* paying in the 1970's and 1980's. To a large extent, their ability to pay cash dividends in the future will determine whether they can provide you with the kind of "plus" you are looking for in Income Plus.

For example, if you are looking for stock investments that will provide you with dependable income and at least a 3% rate of appreciation, averaged over several years, you will be looking for companies with a potential to do well in both good times and hard times. About the only type of companies that can hold their own during hard times are those companies selling products that get used up and have to be replaced—"necessities" and low-priced "indulgences" like chewing gum. Therefore, if you are interested in *dependable* income plus *dependable* appreciation potential, you should concentrate on stock of companies in industries that sell products that get used up fast and are replenished even when family pocketbooks are flat. See page 106 for a list of such industries, which some people call "noncyclical" industries.

By identifying the companies that sell products that need replacing (see tables on pages 100 to 105), you should be able to compile a satisfactory list of Income Plus stocks that will provide you cash dividends plus some protection against both inflation and deflation in the 1970's. In addition, the companies selling everyday items on domestic markets will, for the most part, be little affected by any further devaluations in the 1970's. We might label this group of common stocks as Income Plus—Defensive.

However, if you are desirous of appreciation potentials above the 3% limit that would qualify a stock for consideration in an Income Plus—Defensive portfolio, you will have to be willing to search outside of the noncyclical areas for industries and companies that appear to have

Dependable Cash Dividend Payers that Make Good Candidates for an Investment Objective of Income Plus.†

	DIVIDENDS PAID CONTINUOUSLY SINCE		DIVIDENDS PAID CONTINUOUSLY SINCE
Abbott Labs	1926	Avon Prod.	1919
Adams-Millis	1928	Avondale Mills (ASE)	1904
AFA Protective Systems (O-C)	1889	BMA Corp. (O-C)	1924
Affiliated Publications (ASE)	1882	Baker Oil Tools, Inc.	1929
Airco, Inc.	1917	Balt. Gas & Elec.	1910
Alexander & Baldwin (HON)	1902	Ban Cal Tri-State	1875
Allied Chem. Corp.	1887	Bangor Hydro-Elec. (O-C)	1925
Amerada Hess	1922	Bank of Montreal (MON)	1829
Amer. Bakeries	1928	Bank of N.Y.	1785
Amer. Can	1923	Bank of Nova Scotia (TOR)	1834
Amer. District Telegraph	1903	Bankers Tr. N.Y.	1785
Amer. Elec. Power	1909	Banta, George (O-C)	1927
Amer. Express (O-C)	1870	Baystate Corp. (O-C)	1928
Amer. Gen. Ins.	1929	Becton, Dickinson, & Co.	1926
Amer. Home Prod.	1919	Bekins Co. (O-C)	1923
Amer. Maize-Prod. (ASE)	1929	Belknap Inc. (O-C)	1880
Amer. Natl. Fnl. (O-C)	1923	Bell & Howell	1915
Amer. Natl. Gas	1904	Bell Tel. Canada (ASE)	1881
Amer. Re-Ins. Co. (O-C)	1922	Bemis Co.	1922
Amer. Sec. & Tr. (O-C)	1893	Beneficial Corp.	1929
Amer. Sterilizer	1914	Bird & Son (O-C)	1924
Amer. Tel. & Tel.	1881	Blue Bell Inc.	1923
AMF, Inc.	1927	Book-of-the-Month	1927
Amfac Inc.	1898	Borden, Inc.	1899
Amoskeag Co. (O-C)	1928	Borg-Warner Corp.	1928
Anchor Hocking	1914	Boston Edison	1890
Ancorp Natl. Ser.	1864	Briggs & Stratton	1929
Archer-Daniels-Midland	1927	Bristol-Myers	1900
Aristar	1929	British-Amer. Tob. (ASE)	1928
Arizona Pub. Serv.	1920	British Petroleum	1917
Arrow-Hart (O-C)	1929	Brockton Tauton Gas (O-C)	1922
Arvin Inds., Inc.	1925	Brockway Glass	1927
Atlantic City Elec.	1918	Brown Group	1923
Atlantic Richfield	1927	Burmah Oil Ltd. (O-C)	1930

SPECIAL NOTE ON THE USE OF THIS TABLE

Absence of any company from this checklist must not be taken to mean that it has missed one or more dividends. Every effort has been made to bring this table up-to-date at press time. However, events in the 1970's may bring changes. For instance, Great A&P failed to pay a cash dividend in 1973 for the first time since 1925 and would, therefore, no longer qualify for inclusion on this list. This is a checklist; latest information should be obtained before using this list for current investments.

Dependable Cash Dividend Payers that Make Good Candidates for an Investment Objective of Income Plus.† (cont.)

	DIVIDENDS PAID CONTINUOUSLY SINCE		DIVIDENDS PAID CONTINUOUSLY SINCE
Burroughs Corp.	1895	Cone Mills	1914
Calif. Portland Cem. (ASE)	1909	Conn. Gen. Ins. (O-C)	1867
Cameron Financial	1919	Conn. Natural Gas (O-C)	1851
Campbell Soup	1902	Consumers Gas (TOR)	1848
Canada Malting (TOR)	1928	Consumers Pwr.	1913
Canada Southern Ry.	1887	Continental Bank (Norris-town) (O-C)	1923
Can. Imp. Bank Com. (TOR)	1890	Continental Can Co.	1923
Cannon Mills (O-C)	1890	Continental Corp.	1854
Carolina, Clinch & Ohio	1925	Conwood Corp.	1903
Carpenter Technology	1900	Corning Glass Works	1881
Carriers & Gen. Corp.	1937	Courier Corp. (O-C)	1919
Carter-Wallace Inc.	1883	Courtaulds Ltd. (ASE)	1913
Castle & Cooke, Inc.	1896	CPC Internat'l.	1920
Caterpillar Tractor	1914	Credithrift Fin.	1930
CBT Corp. (O-C)	1924	Crocker Natl.	1926
Ceco Corp.	1921	Crompton Co. (ASE)	1925
Central Hudson Gas & Elec.	1903	CTS Corp.	1930
Central Ill. Light	1921	Dayton Pwr. & Light	1919
Champion Spark Plugs	1919	Delmarva Pwr. & Light	1921
Charter N.Y. Corp.	1865	Deluxe Check Printer (O-C)	1921
Chase Man. Corp.	1848	Dentsply Internatl.	1900
Chattem Drug & Chem. (O-C)	1922	Detroit Ed.	1909
Chem. N.Y.	1827	Diamond Internatl.	1882
Chesebrough-Pond's	1883	Dick (A. B.) Co.	1896
Chessie System	1922	Dillon Cos.	1922
Chrysler Corp.	1926	Discount Corp. N.Y. (O-C)	1920
Cincinnati Bell	1879	Dr. Pepper	1930
Cincinnati Gas & Elec.	1853	Dome Mines Ltd.	1920
Cincinnati Milacron	1923	Dominick Fund Inc.	1930
C. I. T. Financial	1921	Dominion Bank Shares (O-C)	1882
Citizens & Southern Natl. Bank (O-C)	1905	Dom. Foundries & Steel (TOR)	1917
Clark (JL) Mfg. (O-C)	1921	Dominion Textile (MON)	1907
Cleveland Elec. Illum.	1901	Donnelley (R. R.) & Sons	1911
Cluett, Peabody	1923	Dow Chemical	1911
CNA Financial	1913	Dow Jones & Co. (O-C)	1906
Coca-Cola Bottling of L.A. (O-C)	1924	Duckwall Stores (O-C)	1917
		Duke Power	1926
Coca-Cola Co.	1893	duPont	1904
Colgate Palmolive	1895	duPont-Canada (MON)	1912
Columbus & Southern Ohio EL	1927	Duquesne Light	1913
		Eastern Util. Assoc.	1928
Combustion Eng.	1911	Eastman Kodak Co.	1902
Cominco Ltd. (ASE)	1924	Eaton Corp.	1923
Commonwealth Edison	1890	El Paso Elec. (O-C)	1928

Dependable Cash Dividend Payers that Make Good Candidates for an Investment Objective of Income Plus.† (cont.)

	DIVIDENDS PAID CONTINUOUSLY SINCE		DIVIDENDS PAID CONTINUOUSLY SINCE
Emhart Corp.	1902	Girard Co. (O-C)	1837
Equimark Corp.	1872	Gleason Works	1915
Equitable Bancorp (O-C)	1912	Grant (W. T.)	1907
ERC Corp. (O-C)	1915	Gray Drug Stores, Inc.	1928
ESB, Inc.	1901	Gr. Lakes Dredge & Dock	1920
Exxon Corp.	1882	Great Northern Neroosa	1910
Fairmont Foods Co.	1904	Gr. Southern Life Ins. (O-C)	1924
Federal Co.	1926	Guardsman Chem. Coatings (ASE)	1918
Fibreboard Corp.	1923		
Fidelity Corp. of Pa. (O-C)	1926	Gulf Oil Canada (ASE)	1909
Fidelity Union Bancorp.	1893	Hackensack Water Co.	1886
Firestone Tire & Rubber	1924	Handy & Harman	1905
First Amer. Financial (O-C)	1909	Hanover Ins. Co. (O-C)	1853
First Bank System (O-C)	1930	Harcourt, Brace, Jovanovich	1922
First Commercial Bank (O-C)	1841	Harris Bancorp (O-C)	1908
First Empire State (O-C)	1885	Hartford Steam Boiler Insp. & Ins. (O-C)	1871
First Intl. Bankshares	1875		
First & Merchants (O-C)	1869	Hawaii Bancorp (HDN)	1899
First Natl. Bank Boston	1784	Hawaii Corp. (HON)	1916
First Natl. City Corp.	1813	Hawaiian Elec.	1901
First Natl. Holding (GA) (O-C)	1866	Heinz (H. J.) Co.	1911
First Natl. State Bancorp	1812	Heller (WE) Intl.	1921
First Pa. Corp.	1828	Helme Prod.	1912
First Natl. (O-C)	1895	Hercules, Inc.	1928
First Union (O-C)	1919	Hershey Foods Corp.	1930
Fisher Scientific Co.	1909	Hobart Mfg.	1906
Fleming Cos.	1927	Hollinger Min. Ltd. (ASE)	1912
Flickinger (S. M.) Co. Inc. (O-C)	1920	Holmes (DH) Ltd (O-C)	1920
		Home Beneficial CIB (O-C)	1906
Fort Howard Paper	1922	Honeywell, Inc.	1928
Forum Restaurants (O-C)	1930	Hormel (ASE)	1928
Foxboro Co.	1915	Houghton Mifflin Co.	1908
Freeport Minerals	1927	Household Finance	1917
Gamble-Skogmo Inc.	1929	Houston Light & Pwr.	1922
Gannett Co., Inc. (O-C)	1929	Huyck Corp.	1907
Garlock, Inc.	1905	Hydraulic Co. (O-C)	1900
Gen. Amer. Trans.	1919	Idaho Pwr.	1917
General Bancshares	1913	Ideal Basic Inds.	1911
General Cigar	1909	Imperial Cheon Ind ADR (ASE)	1927
General Electric	1899		
General Foods Corp.	1922	Imperial Group (ASE)	1912
General Mills	1898	Imperial Oil (ASE)	1891
General Motors	1915	INA Corp.	1874
Georgia-Pacific	1927	Indiana Natl. Corp. (O-C)	1920
Gillette Co.	1906	Indianapolis Water (O-C)	1926

Dependable Cash Dividend Payers that Make Good Candidates for an Investment Objective of Income Plus.† (cont.)

	DIVIDENDS PAID CONTINUOUSLY SINCE		DIVIDENDS PAID CONTINUOUSLY SINCE
Industrial National	1791	Melville Shoes	1916
Ingersoll-Rand	1910	Mercantile Bancorp. (O-C)	1909
Interco	1913	Meredith Corp.	1930
Intl. Bus. Mach.	1916	Mesta Machine	1914
Intl. Harvester	1910	Midatlantic Banks (O-C)	1805
Intl. Multifoods	1923	Miles Labs, Inc.	1894
Interstate Corp. (O-C)	1928	Mining Safety Appliances (O-C)	1918
Iowa Pwr. & Light	1909	Minn. Mining & Mfg.	1916
Jefferson-Pilot	1913	Mirro Alum.	1902
Jewel Companies (The)	1928	Mobil Oil Corp.	1902
Johnson & Johnson	1905	Mogul Corp. (O-C)	1925
Johnson Service Co.	1901	Monarch Capital (O-C)	1867
Joy Mfg.	1929	Monarch Mach. Tool	1913
Kahler Corp. (O-C)	1917	Monsanto Co.	1925
Kansas City Pwr. & Light	1925	Morgan (J. P.)	1892
Kansas Gas & Elec.	1922	Morton-Norwich-Products	1925
Kansas Power & Light	1915	Mt. States Tel. & Tel.	1911
Keebler Co.	1928	Multimedia Inc. (O-C)	1921
Kellogg Co.	1923	Murphy (G. C.)	1913
Kings Lafayette (ASE)	1890	Nabisco	1899
Kraftco Corp.	1924	Nalco Chem.	1928
Kresge (S. S.)	1913	Nashua Corp.	1926
Kroger Co.	1902	Natl. Fuel Gas	1903
Lane Co. (The) (O-C)	1922	National Standard Co.	1916
Lehman Corp.	1930	Natl. Steel Corp.	1907
Liggett & Myers	1912	Natl. Util. & Ind. (O-C)	1923
Lilly (Eli) & Co.	1885	NCNB Corp. (O-C)	1903
Lone Star Gas	1926	Neonex Intl. Ltd. (ASE)	1930
Louisville Gas & Elec.	1925	New England Merch. (O-C)	1913
Ludlow Corp.	1872	New Engl. Tel. & Tel.	1886
MacAndres & Forbes	1903	New Haven Water (O-C)	1879
Macy (R. H.)	1927	New Yorker Magazine Inc. (O-C)	1929
Madison Gas & Elec. (O-C)	1909	N.Y. State Elec. & Gas	1910
Mangood Corp. (ASE)	1901	NL Industries	1906
Manhattan Life Ins. Gtd. (O-C)	1851	N. N. Corp. (O-C)	1874
Manuf. Hanover	1852	Norfolk & Western	1901
Maple Press (O-C)	1929	Northeast Util.	1927
Marine Bancorp. (O-C)	1928	Northern States Power	1910
Marine Midland Banks	1929	Norton Co.	1922
Marlennan	1923	Nortrust Corp. (O-C)	1896
May Dept. Stores	1911	Noxell Corp. (O-C)	1925
McCormick & Co.	1929	Ohio Casualty (O-C)	1923
Means, F. W. & Co. (ASE)	1928		
Media General CLA (ASE)	1923		
Mellon Natl. Bank Tr. (O-C)	1895		

Dependable Cash Dividend Payers that Make Good Candidates for an Investment Objective of Income Plus.† (cont.)

	DIVIDENDS PAID CONTINUOUSLY SINCE		DIVIDENDS PAID CONTINUOUSLY SINCE
Ohio Edison	1930	Retail Credit Co.	1913
Oklahoma Gas & Elec.	1908	Rexnord	1894
Olin Corp.	1926	Reynolds (R. J.)	1900
Orange and Rockland Util.	1908	Richardson-Merrill Inc.	1922
Otis Elevator	1903	Richmond Corp.	1897
Outlet Co.	1926	Rich's (O-C)	1929
Owens-Illinois	1907	Riggs Natl. Bank (O-C)	1899
Pacific Gas & Elec.	1919	Rochester Tel. Corp.	1926
Pacific Lighting	1909	Rockaway Corp. (ASE)	1928
Pacific Resources (HON)	1912	Rohm & Haas Co.	1927
Pacific Tel. & Tel.	1925	Rosario Resources	1896
Peavey Co. (O-C)	1915	Rose's Stores	1928
Peerless Ins. Co. (O-C)	1915	Safeway Stores	1927
Penn Va. Corp. (O-C)	1916	St. Paul Cos. Inc. (O-C)	1872
Penney (J. C.) Co.	1922	San Diego Gas & Elec.	1909
Pennwalt Corp.	1863	Savannah Food & Ind. (O-C)	1924
Pennzoil United	1925	SCOA Industries Inc.	1929
Peoples Drug Stores Inc.	1927	Scott Paper	1915
Pet Inc.	1922	Scovill Mfg.	1856
Peter Paul	1921	Seattle First Natl. (O-C)	1930
Pfizer Inc.	1901	Security Pac. Natl. Bank (O-C)	1881
Phil. Elec. Co.	1902	Shawmut Assoc. Inc. (O-C)	1837
Phil. Natl. Bank (O-C)	1844	Shell Trans. & Trade	1898
Philip Morris	1928	Sherwin Williams	1885
Pillsbury Co.	1924	Sierra Pac. Pwr. Co.	1926
Pitts Natl. Corp. (O-C)	1867	Singer	1863
Post Corp. (O-C)	1921	Smith, Kline Corp.	1863
Potomac Elec. Pwr.	1904	Sonoco Products (O-C)	1925
PPG Inds.	1899	Sorg Printing (O-C)	1926
Pratt & Lambert (ASE)	1905	South Carolina Ins. (O-C)	1916
Proctor & Gamble	1891	Southeast Banking	1908
Protective Life Ins. (O-C)	1925	Southern Calif. Ed. Co.	1909
Providence Gas Co. (ASE)	1819	Southern Calif. First Natl.	1922
Prov. Life & Acc. Ins. (O-C)	1925	Southern Conn. Gas (O-C)	1850
Prov. Natl. Corp. (O-C)	1865	Southern N.E. Tel.	1891
Public Service of Colo.	1907	Southland Royalty Co. (ASE)	1926
Pub. Ser. Elec. & Gas	1907	Southwest Bancshares (O-C)	1925
Pullman	1867	Southwestern Life Ins. (O-C)	1910
Quaker Oats	1906	Springs Mills	1898
Raybestos-Manhattan	1895	Squibb Corp.	1902
Real Est. Inv. Tr. (ASE)	1889	Stanadyne Inc. (O-C)	1905
Reece Corp.	1882	Standard Brands	1899
Republic Fin'l. Services	1920	Standard Coosa-Thatcher (ASE)	1929
Republic Natl. Bank Dallas (O-C)	1920	Standard Oil Co. Calif.	1912

Dependable Cash Dividend Payers that Make Good Candidates for an Investment Objective of Income Plus.† (cont.)

	DIVIDENDS PAID CONTINUOUSLY SINCE		DIVIDENDS PAID CONTINUOUSLY SINCE
Standard Oil (Indiana)	1894	Union Oil Calif.	1916
Standard Register Co. (O-C)	1927	Union Pacific	1900
Stanley Works (The)	1877	Union Planters Natl. Bank Memphis (O-C)	1927
State St. Boston Finl. (O-C)	1910	Union Special (O-C)	1908
Stauffer Chem. Co.	1915	United Bank Corp. (O-C)	1910
Steel Co. Can. (TOR)	1916	United Illuminating Co.	1900
Sterling Drug Inc.	1902	U.S. Gypsum Co.	1919
SuCrest Corp.	1927	U.S. Bancorp. (O-C)	1899
Sugardale Foods (O-C)	1925	U.S. Tobacco Co.	1912
Sun Chem. Corp.	1929	U.S. Tr. Co. N.Y. (O-C)	1854
Sun Oil Co.	1904	United Va. Bankshares (O-C)	1870
Talcott Natl.	1924	Universal Leaf Tob.	1927
Tampa Elec.	1900	Upjohn Co.	1909
Tasty Baking Co. (ASE)	1915	USM Corp.	1899
Terry Corp. of Conn. (O-C)	1930	Va. Elec. & Pwr.	1925
Texaco	1903	VSI Corp.	1921
Texas Commerce Bancshares	1920	Walco National (ASE)	1890
Texas Util. Co.	1917	Warner-Lambert	1926
Texasgulf Inc.	1920	Wash. Gas Light	1852
Thompson, J. Walter	1917	Wash. Natl. Corp.	1923
TI Corp.	1894	Wash. Water Power	1899
Tiffany (O-C)	1868	Waverly Press (O-C)	1925
Time Inc.	1930	Weingarten (J.) Inc. (O-C)	1928
Times Mirror	1892	West Point-Pepperell	1888
Timken Co.	1921	Weston (Geo.) (TOR)	1930
Todd Shipyards	1916	Westvaco Corp.	1892
Tokheim Corp. (ASE)	1920	Whirlpool Corp.	1929
Toledo Ed. Co.	1922	Whitney Holding (O-C)	1885
Toronto Dom. Bank (TOR)	1857	Wickles Corp. (The)	1895
Towle Mfg. (O-C)	1917	Wiley (John) & Sons (O-C)	1904
Trans-Union Corp.	1914	Williams & Co. (PAC)	1918
Travelers Corp.	1864	Wolverine World Wide	1922
Trico Products (O-C)	1928	Woolworth (F. W.)	1912
Trust Co. of Geo. (O-C)	1930	Wrigley (Wm.) Jr. Corp.	1913
Tucson Gas. & Elec.	1918	Xerox Corp.	1930
UGI Corp.	1885	Youngstown Steel Door	1927
Union Bancorp.	1917	Zale Corp.	1925
Union Carbide Corp.	1918		
Union Elec. Co.	1906		

† All issues traded on New York Stock Exchange unless otherwise indicated:

ASE	American Stock Exchange	MSE	Midwest Stock Exchange
CIN	Cincinnati Stock Exchange	O-C	Over-the-counter
DES	Detroit Stock Exchange	PAC	Pacific Coast Stock Exchange
HON	Honolulu Stock Exchange	TOR	Toronto Stock Exchange
MON	Montreal Stock Exchange		

above-average potentials for the 1970's. If the nation (and its economy) is able to solve some of the problems facing it in the 1970's, there are some obvious industries that should benefit, such as: building materials, cement, electric utilities, energy companies, farm equipment, leisure pursuits, industrial machinery, machine tools, pollution control, and possibly real estate.

Unfortunately, the market has not ignored the potential of the stocks in a number of these industries, having, in some cases, already bid up the prices and dissipated some of the potential for gains in the 1970's. Therefore, if you are interested in companies likely to benefit from our attempts as a nation to come to grips with many of our national problems, you must be prepared to assume some additional risks in the market.

Industries Selling Products That Get Used Up and Replaced

Baking	Insurance
Banking	Medical, dental and hospital supplies
Cans and containers	Natural gas
Cereal foods	Petroleum products
Chewing gum	Photographic supplies
Corn refiners	Shoes
Cosmetics	Soaps
Dairy products	Soft drinks
Drugs and pharmaceuticals	Telephone
Electric utilities	Textbooks
Finance and small loans	Tobacco
Food, canned and packaged	Variety chains
Food chains	
Glass products	

Through careful buying, you may be able to accumulate some of these stocks at attractive prices. But since the companies that will probably interest you the most will be at the forefront of change in the 1970's, their prices may fluctuate more widely than companies selling traditional necessities with proven markets. However, if you limit your selection to those companies with proven ability to generate dependable cash dividends in the past, you should be able to formulate a promising list of candidates that might be called Income Plus—Aggressive.* Like the Income Plus—

* SPECIAL NOTE: When you review the list of dependable income payers in search of buying candidates in the Income Plus—Aggressive category, remember you are looking for companies that are likely to be "problem solvers" in the U.S. and world economies of the 1970's and beyond.

Defensive group, these stocks are dependable cash dividend payers; but unlike the "safer" group, the Income Plus—Aggressive group earns its "plus" with an appreciation potential above the 3% annual rate, hitting somewhere in the 3–5% range, thereby providing you with protection against inflation and leaving a little something over as an extra dividend.

Again, if you are looking for appreciation of 5% or better, you will have to shop outside the dependable income payers. Some of these dependable income payers may also be capable of 5% or better rates of earnings growth, but you are more likely to find good appreciation if you are willing to give up some cash dividend stability. Many companies with higher appreciation potential will be stingy dividend payers since they will be plowing most of their earnings back into the company to achieve its appreciation goals. We might call this group Appreciation Plus stocks—in contrast to Income Plus—with the plus here being some cash dividends or some proven ability to adapt to change in existing markets and introduce new products.

Now, one place to look for better than average appreciation situations in the 1970's is among those companies that have been leaders in the 1950's and 1960's. Not all of these companies will, of course, be able to set as fast a pace in the 1970's as they did in earlier years, but these companies usually have management teams that have been responsive to the rapid change of the 1950's and 1960's so they will at least have some experience in adapting to change. On pages 108 to 110 is a listing of such companies, with proven ability to deliver appreciation.

Entering 1973, several of these companies with proven appreciation records were suffering reversals of fortune and were out of favor with investors, notably stocks in the aerospace, apparel, conglomerates, machine tools, metals, steel, and textiles industries. On the other hand, air transport, chemicals, insurance, and machinery stocks were staging recoveries from earlier reversals. Going into 1974, gold mining stocks, aluminum bands, distillers, forest products, industrial machinery, and domestic oils were the favored groups; meanwhile toys, hotels, apparel, shoes, real estate stocks, publishing, pollution control, leisure-time stocks, air transport, and home furnishings were all experiencing share sell-offs. This ebb and flow is not unusual. In most recent years, industry groups as a whole are exhibiting a "rolling adjustment," with some faltering, others reviving, and yet others continuing to move to new highs with no immediate signs of pause. For the investors in such situations, these advances and retreats offer opportunities for buying and taking profits.

*Companies with Proven Ability to Adapt and Grow**

Aerospace

Boeing
CCI Corp.
Grumman
Rohr Industries
Sunstrand
TRW, Inc.

Air Transport

Braniff Intl.
Delta Air Lines
National Air Lines
Northwest Air Lines
Pan Am World
Western Air Lines

Apparel

Hart, Schaffner & Marx
Kayser-Roth
Munsingwear
Phillips-Van Heusen
V. F. Corp.

Banks

Bank of New York
Chase Manhattan
Cleveland Trust (O-C)
First Bank System (O-C)
Northwest Bancorp
Unionamerica
Valley National Ariz. (O-C)
Wachovia Corp.

Building

Armstrong Cork
Boise Cascade
Corning Glass Works
Evans Products
Fedders Corp.
Georgia-Pacific
Seagrave Corp.
Texas Industries
Thomas Industries

Chemicals

Air Products & Chem.
Emery Industries
Ethyl Corp.
Inmont Corp.
Minn. Min. & Mfg.
Nalco Chem.
National Starch & Chem.
Occidental Pet.
Witco Chem.

Conglomerates

A.J. Industries
Avco
Eagle-Picher
Fuqua Industries
Gulf & Western
Lehigh Valley
Northwest Industries

Cosmetics

Avon
Faberge
Tampax

Department Stores

Assoc. Dry Goods
Broadway-Hale
Federated Dept. Stores
Grant (W. T.)
Interstate Stores
Lane Bryant
Macy (R. H.)
Mays (J. W.)
Mercantile Stores
Sears, Roebuck

Drugs

Amer. Home Prod.
Amer. Hospital Sup.
Baxter Labs
Bristol-Myers
Dart Ind.
Johnson & Johnson
Merck & Co.
Miles Labs
Richardson-Merrell
Rorer-Amchem
Syntex
Warner-Lambert

Electric Utilities

Florida Power
Nevada Power
Tampa Electric

*Companies with Proven Ability to Adapt and Grow** (cont.)

Electronics

AMP Inc.
Burndy Corp.
Emerson Elect.
Hobart Mfg.
Magnavox
Maytag
Texas Instruments
Thomas & Betts
Zenith Radio

Food Products

Beatrice Foods
Carnation
Castle & Cooke
Consol. Foods
Del Monte
Gerber Products
Heinz (H. J.)
Norton Simon
Riviana Foods
Standard Brands

Food Stores

Cook United
Lucky Stores
Stop & Shop

Insurance

Connecticut General (O-C)
General Reinsurance (O-C)
Government Emp. Ins. (O-C)
Republic National (O-C)
Transamerica

Liquor

Brown-Forman "B" (ASE)
Heublein
Walker (Hiram)

Machine Tool

Black & Decker
Skil Corp.
Warner & Swasey

Machinery

AMF Inc.
Bearings Inc.
Briggs & Stratton
Caterpillar Tractor
Chicago Pneumatic
Clark Equipment
Cooper Industries
Crompton & Knowles
Cummins Engine
Dover Corp.
Dravo Corp.
Dresser Industries
Emhart
Fluor
FMC
Gardner-Denver
Halliburton
Harris-Intertype
Koerhing Co.
Leesona
McDermott (J. Ray) & Co.
McNeil Corp.
National-Standard
Ogden Corp.
Parker-Hannifin
Reading & Bates Drilling
Signode Corp.
Textron
U.S. Industries
White Consolidated
Zapata Corp.

Meat Packing

Armour

Metals

Benguet Consol.
Handy & Harman
Hecla Mining
Insilco
McIntyre Porc. Min.
Rosario Resources

Office Equipment

Burroughs
Control Data
Intl. Bus. Machines
Xerox

Paper

Hammermill Paper

*Companies with Proven Ability to Adapt and Grow** (cont.)

Petroleum	*Steel*
Ashland Oil	Carpenter Technology
Clark Oil & Ref.	Kaiser Steel
Getty Oil	
Kerr-McGee	*Telephone*
La. Land & Expl.	Rochester Telephone
Pennzoil Co.	United Telecommunications
Quaker State	
Standard Oil (Ohio)	*Textiles*
Texaco	Burlington Ind.
Union Oil	Collins & Airman
Railroad & Equipment	Duplan
ACF Industries	Indian Head
Pullman	Ludlow Corp.
Soft Drinks	*Variety Stores*
Dr. Pepper	Kresge, S. S.
Royal Crown Cola	Walgreen Co.

* All issues traded on the New York Stock Exchange, unless otherwise indicated.
(ASE) American Stock Exchange
(O-C) Over-the-counter

Unlike the Income Plus group discussed above, the Appreciation Plus group requires more careful watching after purchase. Occasionally, on strong markets, these stocks, attracting investor interest because of their promising appreciation potentials, experience sharp, quick, upward price moves. If you happen to own one of these stocks during such a price surge, you should consider taking your profits by selling. If long-run holding seems warranted, you will probably be able to re-buy later at a more reasonable price after some of the speculative steam has gone out of the market and the stock. No tree grows to the sky and even vigorous expansion often takes a breather. However, if you limit your selections to those companies with proven appreciation potentials, such as the companies listed on the preceding pages, you need not keep as close a watch over your selections as with young, unproven companies that showed promise but had not yet demonstrated any staying power. Stocks selected from among those in the foregoing table (or similar companies) might be called Appreciation Plus—Defensive situations. If you buy these, you will be relying on their proven past managerial abilities to help carry them successfully into the future.

However, if none of these companies that were leaders in the past seems to have, in your opinion, an outstanding potential in the 1970's and beyond, you will be forced to search widely for new companies with new ideas and new products—and even more important, companies that show some indications that they will be able to turn all of this newness into solid, money-making product lines sometime in the 1970's. As you might suspect, these are the companies that are the hardest to find. As a rule, there are no lists that you can screen for the best and most timely buying candidates in this area. If a list of new companies with above-average appreciation potentials is compiled, it generally must be built slowly, one company name at a time, as the result of diligent search and investigation.

Where can you begin, in order to find such companies? One place to look is on the most active list of stocks each day on the NYSE and ASE. Of course, being listed companies, these will not be "new" companies, but they may be "new" companies for most investors, and it is often worthwhile to investigate why they made the most active list. Another place to look is in the financial press—the *Wall Street Journal, Barron's, Forbes,* and other publications featuring stocks. Look particularly for companies whose stock is being bought for the first time by a large mutual fund or institutional investor. Their research staff sees something interesting, so perhaps you should find out more about the company. Another promising source, although time-consuming, is in the various industry trade publications. Sometimes you will find news stories about a company introducing a new product or a new process that would suggest it deserves further attention as a potential candidate for above-average appreciation.

Should you listen to tips? Should you read promotional pieces put out by the brokerage houses praising a stock? By all means listen to tips and read as many of these promotional pieces as you have time to digest, but *never buy solely on a tip or the information contained in an obvious "puff" piece about a stock.* Before you buy, check all of the assumptions that led to this decision to buy yourself. There is another advantage to becoming self-reliant in your ability to make stock buying decisions—you will be in a better position to know when to sell. Knowing *when* to sell is often more important than knowing either what to buy, or even when to buy. Except in the most extreme of bear markets, it is a rare stock that offers no opportunity whatsoever to sell at a higher price after purchase. The problem is deciding when you have made as much profit as you can out of this situation, at least for this time. If you know clearly the reasons for buying, you will have some better grasp of the upside potential and be better able to judge when the rapid appreciation time is over and you should get out.

If you are able to establish firm guidelines for both buying and selling a given stock, your chances of success are enhanced, even if you decide to go after the higher risks and the greater gain potentials that are often present in Appreciation Plus companies that have not been fully seasoned. These situations might be called Appreciation-Plus—Aggressive stocks. They get their added plus not from proven ability, as was the case with Appreciation Plus—Defensive stocks, but from the promise of appreciation potential in the future. There is more risk in Appreciation Plus—Aggressive situations, but there is also more profit potential, if you are willing to take on the research and investigation necessary to uncover such stocks and make a sober appraisal of their prospects.

Regardless of what type of common stock you feel best meets your needs and investment objectives—Income Plus—Defensive, Income Plus—Aggressive, Appreciation Plus—Defensive, or Appreciation Plus—Aggressive—you can clarify your buy and sell decisions by filling out the following worksheet for each common stock you are considering and by maintaining a worksheet for each stock you actually buy.

COMMON STOCK PURCHASE WORKSHEET

Name of Stock ______________________

(1) Purchase Price ______________________

(2) Cash Dividend ______________________
(paid over last 12 months)

(3) Current Yield ______________________
(2 divided by 1)

(4) Earnings, last 12 months ______________________
(per share)

(5) Price/Earnings Ratio ______________________
(1 divided by 4)

(6) Expected Holding Period ______________________
(workout time—months or years)

(7) Expected total cash dividends ______________________
(during workout time, see 6 above)

(8) Expected Earnings ______________________
(per share, during workout time, see 6 above)

(9) Target Selling Price ______________________
(end of workout time, see 6 above)

(10) Investment Objectives in this common stock
(check one)
(a) Income Plus—Defensive ______________

(b) Income Plus—Aggressive ______________
(c) Appreciation Plus—Defensive ______________
(d) Appreciation Plus—Aggressive ______________

(11) Expected Average Annual Return ______________
(Average dividends + average annual appreciation)
(To find average dividends, divide line 7 by number of years in line 6 . . . to find average annual appreciation, line 9 minus line 1 divided by years in line 6)

Using this worksheet, you can quickly compare the workout potentials for all of the common stocks you have under consideration for purchase at any given time. You can sort out your prospective stocks by investment objective (line 10) and determine which stock (or stocks) appears to have the greatest potential for achieving this objective.

This whole discussion so far presupposes one decision; that you want to buy stocks. But you may want to decide whether in fact you do want to buy stocks before you waste your time looking for specific stocks to buy. Should you own stocks in the 1970's? Particularly, should you own stocks if there is likely to be continued inflation, pockets of deflation, and a chance of further devaluation?

First, let us consider the threat of devaluation and its possible effect on stock prices. There have been only three devaluations of the U.S. dollar in history—in 1933, the one announced in December 1971, and the most recent in early 1973. What happened to stock prices after each? In all cases, stock prices rose, at least initially. So, judging by these past performances, stock market traders do not seem to be upset by devaluation. In fact, they seem to assume that a devaluation has bullish implications, perhaps speculating that over the longer haul, devaluation will make U.S. products more competitive abroad and also better able to hold their own on domestic markets.

Over the long-term, continuing inflations should favor holding common stock. In the short-term, however, further inflation in the early 1970's—assuming that our economic policy makers are unable to hit on a strategy that will stop price increases—would have a depressing effect on stock prices. Most investors would be more immediately impressed by the pressure that continued inflation would place upon profit margins and reported earnings by corporations than by the longer-run appreciation potentials for common stocks. Over the long haul, however, common stocks might offset somewhat the erosion in purchasing power as companies have time to adjust their selling prices and costs and learn to live profitably with persistent inflation.

The impact of deflation will depend somewhat on the *type* of deflation experienced in the 1970's. A general deflation, affecting all prices and values in the economy, might, at first, have a stimulating effect on stock prices. Inflation has been billed as the enemy for so long that investors might be encouraged by the prospects of a rollback in prices. In the long run, however, if deflation persisted and continued to erode both prices and values, this would obviously result in lower stock prices.

There is another type of deflation possible. This could take the form of deflation of values in a number of industries and areas of the economy that can no longer compete with other, more dynamic areas of the domestic and international economy. In this case, the deflation may not be widespread enough to result in a general and possibly healthy downward adjustment of prices. Thus, *in*flation, although at a lower rate, could continue to influence most prices; while at the same time, sharp *de*flations of values and prices might affect specific areas of the economy. This prospect would seem to be unfavorable for stock prices, both in the short and long run.

At this point, we might summarize the possible effects of devaluation, inflation and deflation on stock prices in the 1970's, as follows:

Possible Impacts of Conditions in the Economy on Stock Prices in the 1970's

POSSIBLE CONDITIONS IN THE ECONOMY	SHORT-RUN EFFECTS ON STOCK PRICES (EARLY 1970's)	LONGER-RUN EFFECTS ON STOCK PRICES (SECOND HALF OF 1970's)
Devaluation	Favorable	Favorable
Inflation	Unfavorable	Favorable
Deflation (general prices)	Favorable	Unfavorable
Deflation (values and prices in sectors unable to compete)	Unfavorable	Unfavorable

No clear impression of the general direction of stock prices in the 1970's emerges from this analysis. If we assume that there is an equal likelihood of any one of the four conditions in the economy actually happening, then there are two chances that stock prices will rise (favorable) and two that they will fall (unfavorable), in both the short run (early 1970's) and in the longer run (second half of the 1970's).

There appears to be only one way that a generally favorable climate for stock prices can exist in the 1970's. That is: a general price deflation in the early years of the 1970's, followed by an expectation of inflation and rising prices in the last half of the decade. The chances of having a "favorable" climate would be enhanced if there were enough devaluation to make our goods attractive on world markets in the decade.

What are the chances of such an outcome? There are no signs as yet of a general decline in prices in the early years of the 1970's. However, if a general decline in prices did come, an inflationary trend would probably be welcomed by the market in the second half of the 1970's producing a bullish (upward) situation. But there are problems—deflations, defined as general price declines, are often hard to stop once they get started. If deflation comes and persists, then stock prices would fall, after the novelty and early promise of lower prices wore off.

A bearish (downward) 1970's could be created by a failure to stop inflation in the early years of the 1970's, depressing stock prices. This bear trend would carry over into the second half of the 1970's if additional current inflation, on top of the inflation already present from the 1960's, resulted in a sharp collapse of general values and prices.

So a bullish or bearish 1970's would seem to depend on whether price inflation is stopped in the early years of the decade. If it is not, the bears will take command. If inflation is stopped, the bulls have a good chance of taking over.

Prospects for stock prices in the 1970's can also be viewed in other frameworks. For instance, who will want to own common stocks in the 1970's (the demand for stocks)? Will corporations be inclined to issue more common stocks in the 1970's (the supply of stock)?

Over recent years, the small investor has been a net seller of common stocks. The small investor may still be indirectly committed to common stocks, through pension plans, mutual funds, and other forms of institutionalized investment, but his direct ownership of common stocks has declined. It is the institutional investor, chiefly the mutual funds and the pension funds, that have been acquiring this common stock sold by the small investor. Therefore, in the 1970's much depends on whether these institutional investors continue to have large appetites for common stock.

The pension funds, after taking enormous quantities of common stock in the 1960's, seem to be entering a period of slow net growth. The spread of the pension funds, rapid in the 1960's, now appears to have run out of new areas to enter. In addition, withdrawals from existing plans by people retiring in the 1970's will become much larger than in the earlier years when the pension funds were just beginning; very few retiring workers had built up entitlements in the pension funds, or what entitlements they did possess were relatively small because those retirement plans had been established only recently. Hence, the demand for common stocks from this source will be reduced.

Between 1971 and 1973, mutual fund share owners, for the first time in history, redeemed more shares than they bought, reducing the net demand for stocks from this source. Whether there will be net growth in demand for common stocks from mutual funds in the 1970's will depend on whether small investors and others are willing to put more money in than they take out.

Meanwhile, the small investor, usually a reliable customer for common stocks, appears more demoralized and disinterested in the market than at any time since the 1930's. He might be coaxed back into common stocks over the decade, but at the present time, with the newly instituted commission fees higher, especially for smaller orders, the prospects are not bright.

All in all, we might conclude that the over-all demand for common stocks will be softer in the 1970's than was the case in the 1960's.

From the supply side, many corporations may be forced to issue more common stock than they did in the 1960's. At that time, especially in the earlier years when bond rates were lower, corporations relied heavily on debt to finance their expansion. Now, with many corporations pretty well loaned up, they may find it necessary to issue new stock, if they desire added funds for modernization in order to become more competitive and to grow in the 1970's. This is especially true since the interest rate on high grade bonds appear unlikely to get much below 6% for some years. Although 6% yields would be much lower than those prevailing in the late 1960's and early 1970's, 6% is still well above the 4½% rates that prevailed when corporations made wide use of debt for expansion in the early 1960's. So 6% (and higher yield) bonds may help make equity stock issues even more attractive to corporations as a source of funds in the 1970's.

However, this would tend to increase the supply of stocks. And it is difficult to keep prices firm or rising when you increase the supply of anything. This increased supply in prospect for the 1970's seems even more likely to cause stock prices to dip, since, as we have discussed previously, demand is expected to be on the soft side in the 1970's. Both the demand for and the supply of stocks in prospect seem to suggest lower stock prices in the 1970's.

If we bring together the implications of inflation, deflation, and devaluation on stock prices and the prospects for demand and supply of common stock in the 1970's, the scale begins to dip toward the bear side. Even if the economy makes upward progress, the market will be laboring under a number of difficulties of its own, such as slack demand. If the economy makes upward progress, there is a further likelihood that corporations, attempting to get aboard this progress, will ask Wall Street to float more new stock issues, which will be another depressing factor holding down stock prices. At best, it would seem that stock prices will be able to make upward progress only slowly and haltingly in the 1970's. As compared with the 1950's and 1960's, such progress may be interrupted far more frequently by corrections and retracements.

Markets of the 1970's may resemble those of the 1930's more closely than did the markets of the 1950's and 1960's. This does not mean that there will be no profits to be made on the market—even in the 1930's there were several major up and down moves that could have been most profitable for the alert trader. But it does mean that timing may be more important, with frequent reviews of portfolio positions not only desirable but essential. Short-term trading moves may become more frequent and corrections sharper. The market in the 1970's will have to work hard to go uphill, especially if frequent corrections and hesitations show up to add a discouraging note to the proceedings. In short, prices will fluctuate, with any upside trend hard to hold.

While such a market may be discouraging to in-and-out traders, unless they are extremely alert, and may be wearing on the patience of those who take long-term positions and wait for their appreciation, it should bring satisfactory results to those who accumulate through a constant dollar cost averaging plan. Freed from timing worries, investors using a dollar cost averaging plan can accumulate stock at favorable long-term costs even if the market in the 1970's proves highly volatile (see Chapter 12 for a full discussion of dollar cost averaging).

If you should decide to use dollar cost averaging to accumulate a position in common stocks in the 1970's, you might wish to introduce the following rules into your program.

- Whenever high-grade bond yields reach 8% or higher, shift from stocks to bonds.
- If bonds yields then decline, take your profits in the bonds and put the

proceeds into common stocks, increasing the constant dollar amount going into the common stocks at this point. (Remember, from the discussion above, when high-grade bonds yield 8% or better, stock prices in recent years have become labored, having extreme difficulty rising. On the other hand, when money becomes more plentiful and interest rates decline, stock prices usually have had an easier time rising.)

The addition of these two rules to your dollar cost averaging plan will re-inforce the biases of the plan, which force you to accumulate fewer stocks when prices are in a dangerous area and buy more when stocks are relatively low in price.

If the market in the 1970's does prove highly volatile, with upside progress labored, you may wish to consider shorting stocks in times of general market weakness in the 1970's. Short trading is discussed next, in Chapter 15.

CHAPTER 15

Short Selling—The Legal and Occasionally Profitable Way of Selling Something You Do Not Own

It is well known that Wall Street is a two-way avenue (although it is a one-way street). Prices go up and they come down. On average, over an extended time, there are about two trading days with rising prices for every trading day in which prices drop. With more up days than down, you may well ask why the average price of a stock doesn't always rise over time? The answer is quite simple: upside bull moves take longer than sell-offs. Price increases, for the most part, are gradual and take time. Price declines, or bear moves, on the other hand, are usually quick, short, and nasty once they get started. The bears only need one day to reverse what it takes the bulls two days to accomplish.

If you limit your stock purchases to the long side, taking positions only for price rises—that is, buying stocks for their possible appreciation—it is clear that your money will be working with maximum efficiency only about two-thirds of the time. If you wish to take fullest advantage of market swings, you should be on the short side—selling stocks in such a way that you take advantage of their possible decline—at least one-third of the time.

Shorting (selling) a weak stock in a weak market is just as logical as going long (buying) a strong stock in a strong market. Both are simply following the path, or trend, of least resistance at the moment.

Despite the logic, most market investors avoid the short side, limiting their positions to the long side. Adding risk to logic, most investors decide that their nerves cannot stand the short side.

And this wariness of the short side is not without reason. Having taken a long position and paying cash for the position, the very worst that can happen is that the company goes bankrupt and the investor is out his entire commitment. But with short positions, the losses *can be much larger than the funds originally committed.*

When you go short, you in effect sell a block of stock that you do not own at the time. Your broker arranges to borrow this stock for you. Later, when the price declines (assuming a successful short), you replace this borrowed stock with a block purchased at the lower price, your profit being the difference between the price at which you sold the block originally and the price at which you were able to buy the stock for replacement. There are no time limits on the period in which you can be short. However, there are two practical considerations that would suggest that long-term short positions can be unprofitable:

(1) While you are short a stock, if it pays a cash dividend, you must pay this amount to the person from whom you "borrowed" the stock. Even a 25-cent cash dividend means $25 added to your costs if you are short 100 shares.

(2) When you go short, you put up the current price of the stock to demonstrate your ability to replace the stock. Thus, if you short a 40-dollar stock in a round lot (100 shares), you must put up $4,000 plus commissions. If the stock goes down as you expected, fine. But if the stock starts to climb, your broker may ask for more money to assure him that you can replace the stock. If the price goes to 50, you are out $1,000 additional dollars, since it will now cost you $5,000 to replace the 100 shares. With the price at 50, you have to decide whether to cover your short position and take your loss, or risk a longer wait for the collapse you expected. Obviously, if the stock begins to run away, you are in trouble, *there being no upward limit on the amount you can lose.*

Further, although the loss potential is *unlimited* in a short position, the potential gain is *limited.* If you short a stock at 40, the most you can hope to gain is $40 even if the stock goes to zero, which is unlikely (even Penn-Central trades on the NYSE in a 2–5 range after bankruptcy because there are those willing to speculate on the possibility that the rail may eventually work its way out of receivership and become a solvent, operating, profit-seeking company once again). To summarize the difference in gain potential and risk exposure in buying long and selling short:

	LONG POSITION	SHORT POSITION
Potential Loss	100%	Unlimited
Potential Gain	Unlimited	100%

The above table perhaps explains as well as anything the reluctance of most investors to take short positions.

However, there are some special defensive uses of shorts that many investors have found useful. If you "short against the box," that is, short only those stocks that you already own long, then you do not run unlimited risks, since if you cannot replace the stock at a reasonable price you can always surrender the stock you already own.

But why would you want to short a stock that you already own long? Tax considerations are at least one reason. Suppose that you have a stock in which you have a large profit. However, it is December, near the end of the tax year, so you wish to defer the profit from sale until the next year, but you are afraid that the stock may decline before you can make a timely sale in terms of your tax situation. In this case, you can short the stock, hold your long position, and close out both positions in the next year, thus qualifying at least your capital gains from your long-position for more favorable tax treatment. If the stock declines, you will make less on your long position than you would have by selling now, but with a short position as well, you will gain on the short sale.

There are other possible defensive uses of shorts, especially in hedging operations, but for most investors selling short is a doubtful operation for several reasons:

- You will have to know something about market timing to sell short. Most traders short only in bear markets, feeling that the chances of profit are slim in a bull market that is exerting upward pressure on all stocks, even stocks in ill-run, poorly functioning companies.
- Even in weak markets, you should short only weak stocks. Bear markets often have "reversals," and in such markets glamour stocks and former trading favorites often stage brief, if abortive, rallies, which could upset your short position.
- Never short a stock that has a "thin" market. Sometimes, the market

supply is "thin" because the company has only 1 or 2 million shares outstanding. In other cases, large blocks of a 5 or 6 million share issue may be closely held by family members, other corporations or institutional holders. In this case, if you short, you may walk into a "bear trap," that is, few will be willing to sell you the stock in the event it goes against you, meaning that you pay an extremely high price just to cover your short position.

All things considered, shorting, except for shorting against the box for defensive purposes, is probably best left to the professionals.

However, if you decide to sell short, your decision can be clarified by filling out the Short Selling Worksheet below.

SHORT SELLING WORKSHEET

Name of Stock ____________________

(1) Selling Price ____________________

(2) Cash Dividend and
Date of Next Payout ____________________

(3) Number of Shares Outstanding ____________________

(4) Number of Shares Closely Held ____________________

(5) Behavior of Stock in Last 12 Months:
(a) Rising, actively traded ____________________
(b) Flat, or Down, low volume ____________________

(6) Downside Potential
(a) Workout Time, estimated ____________________
(b) Downside Target ____________________

Assume that you have established to your satisfaction that the market trend is bearish (down). Then if (2) in the table above is small; (3) is large (more than 3 million shares); (4) is small relative to (3), and you check (5b) rather than (5a), you will have a possible short candidate. If (6a) is a relatively small time span and (6b) is well below (1), your short may work for you.

There is another far safer way to profit from a possible slide in the price of a stock. This is called a "put," which is one strategy for making your money do more for you with less. We turn to these strategies now.

CHAPTER 16

How to Go Long and Short with Less Funds—Margins, Convertibles, Warrants, Puts and Calls

In the market, when a little will do a lot, leverage is present. If you can borrow, for example, you can make a *little* of your *own* money do a lot in the market. Or if you can get an option to buy more securities, you can often make a *little* command a *larger amount* on the market. Either way, for the same amount of outlay, you can increase your profits using leverage in your investing.

Let's deal with borrowing first. One of the most accessible types of leverage available to the average investor is in a margin account. If you buy on margin, you put up only part of the total purchase price of a block of stock, your broker lends you the rest. The amount you have to put up is subject to regulation by the Federal Reserve and varies with business conditions.

Here's how it works. Suppose stocks can be purchased on a 55% margin. This means that you can command $10,000 worth of common stock by putting up $5,500 in cash, with your broker lending you the remaining $4,500. Of course, he will charge you interest on the loan (see Chapter 6, item 8, for a discussion of margin account charges).

But despite interest charges, the advantages of a margin account are great. Without margin, you could buy 110 shares of a $50 stock with $5,500;

but with $5,500 on margin, you could buy 200 shares of the same stock. If the stock goes to 60, you would make $1,100 if you had bought 110 shares outright, or a 20% return on the $5,500 invested. However on margin, the profit would be $2,000 on 200 shares, or over 36% on the same $5,500 of your own money. Of course, there would be a small deduction for the interest on the borrowed funds, say $40, depending on how long it took the stock to move from 50 to 60. But the essential point is that, by using margin, you are able to almost *double* your profits when you can borrow up to 45% of the initial outlay required.

As you might suspect, there are some added risks with margin. First, if the stock being margined long goes down instead of up, your broker will call for more margin (to cover the loss that might be entailed if the stock were to be sold before the price went up). If you do not put up more money, he will be forced to close out your account and charge you for the loss. Second, if the broker should fail, or go out of business while your margin account is active, it will create problems for you. Since he is lending you money, he holds the stock as collateral. If you owned the stock outright, paying the full price, you could minimize the risk of failure by having the broker ship you the stock rather than leave it in your account in a "street" name, that is, he holds the stock for you instead of mailing the stock certificate to you. So if you open a margin account, you should investigate your broker more closely than you would, perhaps, with a regular account.

There are ways to protect yourself against either a margin call or a failure of the broker and still use margin. Many traders, whether they are long or short, use a 10% rule in trading. If either a long or a short goes 10% against them, they close out the position, cutting their losses short, and try again. These traders reason that a 10% move in the wrong direction indicates that either their assumptions or the timing are wrong. Either way, it pays to get out before the losses mount. There is a generally sound market maxim: Never meet a margin call. Using the 10% rule when you buy stock on margin, short or long, will prepare you to live under this rule.

If you are wary of leaving your stock in a street name on margin, you might consider paying cash for the stock and then taking it to a bank and using it as collateral for a loan. If you leave the stock with the banker, he will probably charge you 7–9% for the loan, or very close to what your broker will charge you for margin. Legally, you cannot use this borrowed money to buy more stocks. However, this money borrowed with your stocks as collateral can free other funds, leaving your over-all borrowing picture about the same as if you had a loan from the broker.

The only advantage bank borrowing has over a loan from the broker is that you have greater control over the stock. Essentially, the question is whether you trust your banker more than you trust your broker. If either were to close up, you would suffer delays in getting control over your stock again. Since the broker is prepared to lend you margin money as a routine of his daily business, it would be more convenient to find a broker you can trust, if you wish to margin stock.

However, if you wish to borrow against bonds, the bank will offer you a larger margin. Just how much you can borrow against bonds as collateral at a bank will depend on the type of bond—U.S. government bonds generally being the best—and on your relationship with the bank. But a bank will generally lend anywhere from 70% to 95% of the market value of quality bonds; whereas at a broker, in a margin account for bonds, you will get only the amount allowed for common stock at the moment, say 45% when the margin requirement is 55%. (Margin requirements are subject to change. They are controlled by the Federal Reserve System as part of their general powers to regulate the money supply.)

Borrowing is only one type of leverage in the market. Buying options is another. Investors can increase their profit potential with fewer dollars committed by buying options on common stock—in such forms as rights, warrants, convertibles—and on puts and calls. All of these options give you the right to buy or exchange one type of paper or contract, for the common stock of a company. Often, these options permit you to acquire the common stock on more favorable terms than you can get on the market.

We will examine convertibles first. Convertible bonds and convertible preferred stocks offer the investor two features: (1) the added security and assured yields of a senior security, and (2) the option to convert into the common stock at stated prices. Generally, the effective conversion price is above the current market price, so these issues give the investor, in most cases, a future call on the stock. For instance, a $1,000 par bond yielding 6% return may be convertible until maturity into 20 shares of the common. This would be an effective price of $50 ($1,000 divided by 20). If the common is selling at $35 currently, it will obviously not pay to convert ($35 times 20 = $700). If the common sells at $53, it still may not pay to convert, even though 20 shares of the common at $53 would be worth $1,060, since by converting, the investor would lose his $60 annual interest. But as the bond nears maturity, prices above $53 become more attractive, since the bond holder will get back only $1,000 on maturity. And at almost any time, a $75 stock price might make conversion attractive ($75 times 20 = $1,500), if it offsets the $60 annual interest to be earned each year on your bond to maturity. Much depends on whether the common pays a cash dividend.

Some investors are impressed by the hedge provided by convertibles—when the common is moving up, the convertible tends to move with the common; when the common is depressed, the yield offered by the convertible offers some downside protection, with the bond features taking over.

Listed convertibles can be bought on margin, up to the amount available on common stocks at brokers or banks currently. However, high quality convertible bonds traded Over-the-Counter (OTC) can still be margined at banks on more favorable terms than at brokerage houses. Unless money is extremely tight, bankers are usually willing to lend up the 75% or 80% on quality OTC convertibles. This is the only extra leverage available currently in convertibles, as opposed to common stocks.

These, then, have been the general features of convertibles that have attracted investors to them in the past. Now it is time to ask a more pertinent question: Are convertible issues attractive for the 1970's?

If your investment objective is maximum current income, the answer is no. Convertibles generally sell to yield less than straight bonds. For current income, you will do better in straight bonds (see Chapter 9).

What if you are seeking assured income *plus* appreciation? Again the answer is no. There are very few convertible issues with a rating of A or better (see Chapter 9). So, in most cases, you must be willing to assume additional risk to buy convertibles. Many of the more attractive convertibles were selling in early 1974 at a premium, with much of this premium reflecting speculation in the common stock. Market corrections will wring this speculative water out fast, locking you in with only moderately attractive current interest payments. So your income is less certain than in straight bonds, and the upside appreciation potential appears doubtful.

When should you buy convertibles in the 1970's? Only during severe market corrections. In general, the best time to buy a convertible is near the bottom of a bear market, or in the early stages of a recovery. Here the appreciation potentials are the greatest. In the context of the 1970's, this means that convertibles would make attractive long-term investments only on major market corrections. With the Dow at 850 or above, a "major correction" would mean a decline to somewhere in the range of 675 to 725 on Dow-Jones industrial index. In this range, the Dow would be trading near the tops of the late 1950's and early 1960's, where technical analysis would suggest that some support should be coming into the market. At 700 on the Dow, the 30 industrials would be selling to yield around 5.2% and at about 8.5 times earnings, based on 1973 cash dividends and earnings per share. If these increase by 10% in 1974–1975, at 700 the Dow industrials would still be yielding only about 5.7% or only slightly above the yields available on Series E Savings bonds, and selling at around 7¾ times earnings, or approximately the price investors were willing to pay for earnings in the late 1940's and early 1950's.

Even at 700 on the Dow, caution should be used in accumulating convertibles for long-term holding. Back in the late 1940's and the early 1950's—the last time market investors generally were anticipating serious business reversals, with some expecting a resumption of the depression of the 1930's—the Dow industrials were selling to yield 6–8% and at *less* than 10 times earnings. So 5% yields or better and 10 times earnings or less, even assuming continued improvement in the 1970's, may not prove a solid support area if investors undergo a sharp reversal in confidence and come to expect (and discount) a major depression later in the 1970's.

In sum, during the 1970's, defer any long-term commitments in convertible bonds or convertible preferred stocks until the market has tested and successfully rebounded from the 675 to 725 range of the Dow industrials. Even if this test of lower ranges is deferred, stock markets in the 1970's are likely to be nervous and subject to sharp swings. On such markets, convertibles, with thinner markets than the common and larger initial outlays required, appear less flexible or suitable vehicles than the common until a sharp market correction has brought them into better buying ranges.

Rights offerings and warrants are another way of getting access to common stock for less initial outlay.

Rights offerings, as opposed to warrants, are usually short-term options—a few weeks at most—to buy the common stock of a company. They are issued to current stockholders, usually one right per share held. These right offerings entitle the holder to purchase common stock at a price below the going market price—at the so-called subscription price. (Often, it takes several rights to buy a share of stock. Also, if the current stockholder does not wish to use his rights, he may sell them on the market.)

There are several advantages in using rights to acquire common stocks:

- The subscription price is below the market price.
- No commissions are charged when the stock is purchased.
- These issues can be bought in a "special subscription" account, which permits purchase with roughly 25% cash.

Warrants are rights offerings of longer duration, usually giving their holders a call on the common at a specified price for *several years,* or in some cases even perpetual calls. However, warrant subscription prices, unlike rights, are generally set *above* the market price of the common at the time of issue. On the market, price movements of warrants usually reflect quite closely the trading movements of the higher-priced common stocks on which the holders of the warrants have a call. Moving with the common but costing less than the common, warrants are leveraged and offer a way to command more common stock for less outlay. In effect, they work like a margin account, but they avoid the interest charges on the debit balance and the concern about a margin call.

Should you buy warrants in the 1970's? As a general rule, you should not buy a warrant unless you would be willing to buy the common. Historically, low-priced warrants have higher appreciation potentials than do higher-priced ones. In terms of timing, warrants generally have their greatest appreciation potential on the upswing from a major market bottom. In the 1970's, this would mean that warrants would be most attractive *after* a rebound is *well underway* from a test of the 675 to 725 range of the Dow industrials (see the discussion earlier in this chapter of this point). Warrants, offering no voting rights and no cash dividends, appear to have only speculative appeal as possible vehicles for in-and-out trading on the numerous rallies and reversals that are likely on the nervous markets of the 1970's. They are certainly not for buying and holding in the 1970's, unless they become available at rock-bottom prices on severe market corrections —corrections that carry well below the 675 to 725 test range on the Dow industrials.

Now, even though warrants may become attractive in the 1970's on steep market dips, not all stocks have warrants outstanding. In fact, there are only a handful of stocks with warrants at the present time. However, puts and calls permit the investor to acquire tailor-made options to buy almost any common stock actively traded on markets.

A put or a call is a contract between an option writer (or seller) and an option holder (or buyer). A call gives the option holder the right to buy from the writer a specified number of shares (usually 100) of a security at a stipulated price (called the "striking price") for a specific period, usually six months or longer. A put is just the opposite of a call, giving the holder the right to sell 100 shares (typically) of a stock at a specified striking price to the writer at any time during the term of the contract. A call is purchased if you desire to go long, a put permits you to speculate on a price decline and is an alternative to shorting a stock.

Calls typically are bought for about 10–20% of the current market price of 100 shares of the common, with the price of the stock, the volatility of the stock in recent trading, and the length of time for which the call contract is being written all affecting the price. When you buy an option, the purchase price goes to the writer of the option as a fee, with you having no further claims to this money. Whether you execute the call or not, this fee is a cost of trading in the option.

For example, suppose you buy a call, paying $350 on 100 shares of a common stock at a striking price of 20, good for six months. This means that during the next six months you have the right to buy 100 shares at $20 a share from the writer who sold you the option. If in the six months, the stock never trades above 20, you do not call and lose $350. If the stock, within six months, goes to 30, it will pay to call the stock at 20. You then pay the writer $2,000 for the stock as per your option with him, and you then can sell them on the open market for $3,000. Ignoring commissions, this is a gross profit of $1,000, or a net profit of $650 after deducting the cost of the option.

The advantages of call option leverage in contrast to other strategies can be illustrated as follows:

Profit Results, Assuming Different Methods of Financing the Purchase, when 100 Shares of a $20 Stock Goes to $30

TAKING A POSITION USING:	PROFIT*	PERCENTAGE RETURN ON CASH RISKED
$2,000 in cash	$1,000	50.0%
$1,100 in cash on 55% margin	$1,000	90.9%
$350 in cash for call option	$ 650	185.7%

* Ignoring commission costs and interest on margin account

It is clear from the table that if the stock goes up, the $350 call option offers the best return.

But what happens if the stock goes down? Under the call option, your loss is clear—it is exactly the $350 price paid for the option. How does this compare with the other strategies?

If you buy on margin, the costs depend on your trading rules. Let us assume that you are using a 10% rule, closing out your position when a long goes down by 10%. This would mean a sale at 18, or a loss of $200. Roundtrip commissions and interest on the money borrowed on margin would add about $115 to your expenses, for a total of $325, which is very close to the $350 option price. Of course, if you did not use the 10% rule, and the stocks sank further, your losses could be even greater, possibly resulting in a margin call.

With an outright purchase, using $2,000 cash, you could of course continue to hold even though the price declined. However, your "costs" would depend on how long this sinking stock tied up your funds. Suppose you waited two years for a comeback in this $20 stock. If it paid no cash dividends, your costs of waiting would be the money lost for alternative uses of your $2,000 tied up. Even if this $2,000 had earned only 5% in a savings account, the two-year loss in interest would be $205, compounded, and $315.25 if it took three years, which is again close to the $350 option price.

To summarize, *call options,* as compared with cash positions and margin buying, *are superior if the stock moves in the direction you expect,* delivering a higher return on the cash committed. On the other hand, *the costs of a call option are often very close* to those associated with cash or margin positions *when the stock moves against you.*

Much the same demonstration could be made for puts, as compared with going short. However, the results would be even *more favorable* for puts, as compared with short positions, for two reasons:

(1) Puts, reflecting market traders' bias against going short, are generally available at lower prices than calls. Puts are often available at 8–15% of the current market price of 100 shares of the common, as compared with 10–20% for calls. This means that the comparative costs of puts and cash or margin positions in short trades would be even closer than was the case with calls.

(2) Puts eliminate one of the most risky aspects of taking a short position—the chance of almost unlimited loss. With a short, you are forced to chase a run-away stock until you can cover (see Chapter 15). But with a put, you can take advantage of a possible period of weakness in a stock with your *total loss exactly predetermined*—it will be the price you paid for the put, no more or less, regardless of what happens to the stock on the market. If the stock goes down in price, you execute your put, getting a better return than you could on either a cash or margin position on the short side. If the stock goes up in price, you have your loss, limited to the option price, and no worries about how and when to cover.

In the 1970's, puts and calls offer the best vehicle for in-and-out trading. If you wish to accumulate and hold, dollar cost averaging, of course, is best suited for the 1970's (see Chapter 12). But if you wish to assume the added risks of quick in-and-out trading, puts and calls offer many advantages, for either short or long positions:

- Put and call contracts are flexible in terms of the time period, making them suitable for the nervous markets of the 1970's. Most of these options are written for six months, and you will be doing well if you can hold six months of market movements in your sights in the 1970's. In the 1970's, if you cannot see a trading profit within a six-month horizon, you should not be trading at all.
- If a position moves in the direction you expect, up for longs and down for shorts, puts and calls usually provide about *twice* the profit potential of a margin position (if margins are around 50%, or higher) and *three times* the profit potential of a cash position.
- If a position goes against you, the amount of your loss is precisely limited by the price you paid for your option and in many cases is no more than you would lose using margin or all cash. And the option price can be treated as a capital loss for tax purposes.
- Puts and calls offer greater flexibility and range than do rights, warrants, or convertibles since they can be tailor-made for almost any actively traded stock and are not dependent on a company management's decision to make them available for investors.
- Puts are especially attractive, being lower in price than calls and exposing their buyer to less risk than he would assume in a short position.

Before buying a put or a call, fill out the following worksheet. It will help clarify your plan for making profits through in-and-out trading.

OPTION PURCHASE WORKSHEET

Type of Option __________

(1) Cost of Option __________

(2) Selling Price of Security Options __________

(3) Points the Security Price Must Move to Pay for Option (divide (1) by the number of shares optioned, usually 100) __________

(4) Time Remaining in Option ______________________

(5) Target Price for Security Optioned (within time limits of (4) above) ______________________

(6) Gross Profit ______________________
(5 minus 2)

(7) Net Profit (6 minus 1) ______________________

Clearly, the two critical numbers in the Option Purchase Worksheet are (3), the points the stock must move to pay for the option, and (5) the expected price to be reached by the stock within the time limits of the option. For example, if you pay $1,000 for a six-month call on 100 shares of a $70 stock, the stock must move up at least 10 points to pay for the option (1,000 divided by 100). Described another way, you do not begin to profit until this stock has moved up at least 10 points. Therefore, the target price in (5) will indicate the amount of profit you can expect.

If you have no reason to think that the stock can appreciate by more than 10 points in the next six months, then you should not buy the call. Also, you should not margin the stock—you are likely to be out at least $1,000 if the stock moves against you, forcing you to close out at a loss, or to face a margin call. If you are attempting to profit from in-and-out trading, you should also probably avoid a long position, using cash, since the stock will most likely prove to be a time-waster, tying up your money and delivering what will prove to be an unsatisfactory trading profit for the time involved in the position.

Two additional notes on puts and calls: First, if in-and-out trading, using puts and calls, appears too risky for you in the 1970's, you may still be able to profit from the puts and calls markets by becoming a *writer* of these contracts rather than a seller. An SEC study shows that only about 20% of all puts and calls are ever executed, underlining the extreme risk in this type of trading. But, for the writer, there is the fee, which is his to keep and spend from the moment the contract is written.

If you have a portfolio of stocks, you might consider writing puts and calls. Contact a put and call broker. He will be glad to tell you whether the stocks in your portfolio appear suitable for writing these contracts. There is little risk—the worst that can happen to you is that you will have to deliver or accept 100 shares of a stock. If you own the stock, a call is no problem. If you write a put, you can defend yourself by shorting the stock if it really falls out of bed (see Chapter 15).

Second, in March 1973, the Chicago Board of Trade, the world's largest commodity exchange, opened a central exchange for puts and calls. Although puts and calls have been traded for years, this was the first time that a central clearing for these options was available to investors. Trading started small, being limited to only 16 actively traded New York Stock Exchange issues. By the end of 1973, the Chicago Board expanded this trading to 32 active NYSE issues. Two hundred (or more) such options are eventually to be offered. Other exchanges are watching developments in option trading closely. If they prove successful, trading will most likely be extended to other exchanges. If you are interested in puts and calls, watch developments on these new option markets for trading opportunities. If successful, they should help broaden and strengthen the trading in options.

If you feel that you have neither the time, the inclination, nor the talent for wrestling with the problems of forecasting the target price for a stock over a six-month period, then you should avoid in-and-out trading, limiting your investment program to long-term accumulation through dollar cost averaging (see Chapter 12). Or consider turning over the decision-making for your investment portfolio to professional managers. The choices open to you in getting someone else to manage your investment portfolio are discussed in the next chapter.

CHAPTER 17

Mutual Funds—Should You Leave the Driving to Others?

If the guidelines suggested in the foregoing Chapters 14 through 16 for managing a portfolio of securities, either for long-term holding or in-and-out trading, appear too complex, you may wish to consider letting someone else manage your investment portfolio. If reading the financial pages of the daily newspaper is sheer drudgery for you, then you will probably be better off letting an outsider take over. It is true that self-reliant investors are usually better off, especially in times of rapid change such as are likely to be present in the 1970's. But self-managed portfolios that are handled in a slapdash offhand manner will often collapse like a house of cards in a strong, adverse wind. While the out-of-pocket costs may be minimal if you manage your own portfolio, if you feel that you are likely to do a poor job, the price of do-it-yourself investing can be quite high.

What will it cost you to relieve yourself of the tedium (and possible price) of a self-managed portfolio? There are a growing number of personal money managers willing to consider portfolios of around $50,000 and less. These professional managers generally charge an annual fee of about 1½% per $1,000 of the funds managed. For $25,000, this would be $375, regardless of how the portfolio performed. Only long-term experience will tell whether the results will justify this outlay.

If these charges are more than you would be willing to pay for professional handling of your portfolio, you can consider such non-personal managers of your funds as load or no-load mutual funds, and closed-end funds. All of these fund managers pool the assets of investors and seek income, appreciation, and other goals by investing these assembled funds in common stocks, bonds, and other securities.

Both load and no-load mutual funds are "open-end" funds, that is, they continuously issue new fund shares as investors place their money for management in the individual fund. Closed-end funds, on the other hand, manage a fixed pool of assets, with new investors having to buy their shares from other investors already in the fund. Closed-end funds are often traded on the NYSE and ASE, with the cost of buying and selling being simply the regular commission charges for common stock.

Load funds, on the other hand, have salesmen who aggressively pursue new investors for the fund. Generally, new investors must pay about an 8% fee, or "load," for buying into the fund. This 8% fee is split between the salesman and the fund organizers. In addition, some fund managers get a fee for managing the investment portfolio (about 0.5% of the amount managed). These charges are taken off the top before calculating the per-share earnings of the fund. There is no charge for redeeming the shares, which the holders are free to do on any day the market is open.

No-load funds, however, make no charges for buying into the fund. There are no salesmen, the buyer having to seek out the fund rather than being "sold." As a result, the total amount of funds managed by no-load funds tends to be smaller than those managed by most load funds. This is not necessarily a disadvantage, since often fund portfolio managers can do a better job managing smaller sums than larger sums. Of course, these fund managers charge a fee for managing the portfolio, which is generally about the same as the management fees in load funds, about 0.5% of the total amount managed. In addition, some no-load funds also charge a small fee for redeeming the shares. But this fee is well below the 8% load charged by the load funds, and perhaps even more important, it comes at the end, not the beginning, of the investment program.

The difference is important. If the load is taken off the front, then the investor's position is permanently reduced. This can be seen clearly in the following example, where we assume that a load and a no-load fund both perform equally well (that is, score the same increases in net asset value per share). The example shows that the investor in the load fund would always be behind because of the 8% front-load. When $1,000 is invested in a no-load fund, the full $1,000 goes to work immediately, but with an 8% load fee, only $920 goes to work immediately, with the consequences shown in the table.

10-Year Results of Investing $1,000 in a Load and a No-Load Fund, Assuming Equal Performance by Each of the Funds.

IF NET ASSET VALUE RISES AT A COMPOUND RATE OF: (ASSUMING ALL DIVIDENDS REINVESTED)	10-YEAR GAIN NO-LOAD FUND ($1,000 INVESTED IN FIRST YEAR)	10-YEAR GAIN LOAD FUND (ONLY $920 INVESTED IN FIRST YEAR)
5%	$1,628.89	$1,498.58
10%	$2,594.00	$2,341.48
15%	$4,046.12	$3,722.32

It is clear that the load investor suffers as a result of not having the $80 at work from the beginning. At 5%, the 10-year disadvantage is $130.31. As the annual average gain assumed for both funds increases, the disadvantage of the load investor increases, reaching $323.68 at a 15% compound growth rate. Of course, the indicated advantages of a no-load fund should be "burdened" with the selling fees. They are typically 1–2% of the value of the shares sold. This would mean a $16 to $32 subtraction from the $130.31 net advantage when the appreciation rate is 5%, and between $40 and $80 when the appreciate rate is 15%—or a net advantage of between $243.68 and $283.68. Even after subtracting the selling fees, the average annual appreciation in a no-load fund is between 1% and 2½% better over a 10-year period because 8% *more* of your money begins to work for you from the very first year that you buy into the fund.

Similarly, closed-end funds would also be at a disadvantage, as compared with no-load funds, since the brokerage fees charged to buy in would be subtracted from the total funds at work for the investor. (In 1972, for instance, the SEC found that the commissions on closed-end funds worked out to about 7.9%.)

But costs are only one side of the decision to buy; the other side is the performance expected from the funds. On the basis of the past record, closed-end funds come in a poor third. Their performance as a group has lagged well behind both load and no-load funds. Among the load and no-load funds, there is a wide divergence in results, some individual funds performing well, even brilliantly, while others have turned in dismal records. And there is little year-to-year consistency in results—a fund can lead the parade in one year and slip to number 387 in performance results in the very next year. But *as between load and no-load funds, there is absolutely no evidence to suggest that load funds perform better on average than do no-load funds.* Since no-load funds cost less, there appears to be no reason whatsoever for buying a load fund, when no-load funds are readily available.

Of course, you will have to seek out a no-load fund on your own. There are some 140 no-load funds in existence. You can get a complete, up-to-date listing of these no-load funds by writing to the No-Load Mutual Fund Association at 375 Park Avenue, New York, N.Y. 10022. With this list, you can then contact the funds. They will send you a prospectus and explain how you can buy shares. After reading over the materials sent you, you will be in a position to select the fund that appears best suited for your investment objectives.

To help you in selecting a fund, you might fill out the following worksheet. You may also wish to use the worksheet to check out some load funds just to make certain that their performance potentials are no better than those available in the no-load funds you are considering.

MUTUAL FUND SHARES PURCHASE WORKSHEET

Name of Fund ____________________

Objective of Fund ____________________
(income, capital gains, etc.—
stated in the prospectus)

(1) Purchase Price ____________________

(2) Buying Fees, if any ____________________

(3) Redemption Fees, if any ____________________

(4) Estimated Income Dividend ____________________

(5) Estimated Capital Gains Dividend ____________________

(6) Estimated Annual Appreciation ____________________
(assuming all dividends re-invested)

Once you have selected a suitable no-load fund for immediate investment, or accumulation, you might consider purchasing these shares using dollar cost averaging (see Chapter 12). If you feel that the problems of selecting a common stock (or stocks) for a systematic investment program, as outlined in Chapter 14, are too great for you to overcome on your own, you might well consider using your no-load fund as your common stock commitment. Professional managers will assure you wide diversification, periodic review of holdings, and sale and re-purchase in an effort to improve performance, so their supervision may prove superior to yours over time, especially if your interest is slight and your commitment only half-hearted.

There is one last investment area that needs to be discussed—commodities. We turn to that now.

CHAPTER 18

Commodity Trading—A Fast Track if You Are in a Hurry

If the discussion of in-and-out trading, using puts and calls, in Chapter 16, whetted your appetite for more trading opportunities in the 1970's, then you might consider commodity trading. On the other hand, if the discussion of in-and-out trading failed to attract your interest, you may safely skip this chapter.

On commodity markets a wide variety of raw materials are bought and sold for future delivery—grains, soybeans, silver, potatoes, coffee, platinum, orange juice, etc. Producers of these commodities (farmers, metal fabricators, etc.) and users of these commodities (food processors, bakers, manufacturers, etc.) use these markets to reduce the risks from an unexpected rise or fall in the prices of the commodities they produce or use. Individual investors are also free to trade in these markets.

The unit of trading on commodity markets is called a contract, which is the minimum amount that may be bought or sold. What constitutes a contract varies from commodity to commodity. For example, a wheat contract currently is for 5,000 bushels; a cotton contract is for 50,000 pounds; a platinum contract for 50 ounces; a cocoa contract for 30,000 pounds. These contracts are for specific months in the future when the seller is obliged to make the quantity of the commodity in the contract available to the buyer.

Individual investors trading exclusively for speculative profits hopefully never see the actual goods being contracted for. Commodity speculators, as opposed to potential users of these commodities, are interested solely in the trading profits available from buying and selling commodity contracts. They buy a contract in the hopes of a price rise before the indicated delivery date. They sell contracts when they feel that prices for the future delivery month covered in the contract are at their highest—if they are right and prices do actually fall before delivery date, then they can complete the transaction by buying at a lower price and selling it at the higher price already agreed on under the terms of their contract.

Commodity trading more closely resembles bond and stock trading than any other form of investment.

But in commodities there is no equivalent to the long-term, buy-and-hold of stock trading. So there is no other alternative in commodities but in-and-out trading. There are no dividends, rents, or royalties, the only profit being from the rise and fall of prices while contracts are held long and short. There are several special features of commodity trading that, over the years, have lured traders from the floor of the stock exchanges to the commodity pits.

Perhaps the most appealing feature of commodity trading is the leverage available. Margins of only 5% to 10% of the contract value are common in commodities, well below the requirements for common stocks where margins have never been less than 50% in the years since World War II. The margins for commodities are, in effect, good-faith deposits to protect the broker rather than down payments.

Trading costs are also low, relative to the value of the contract. "Round turn" commissions for wheat on the Chicago Board of Trade are $22, for instance, with a contract consisting of 5,000 bushels, worth about $7,750 when wheat sells at $1.55 a bushel. There are no interest charges in the margin accounts. Speed and accuracy of executions of orders is as good as on the stock exchanges.

There is little hidden about the factors that may influence commodity prices. Important political and economic information that may affect commodity prices is generally available to all traders on an equal footing. Much of the vital supply and demand information from the growing and producing areas is available in reports from U.S. government agencies and bureaus, especially the U.S. Department of Agriculture. There is no board of directors of Wheat, Inc. that can make decisions in secret. As compared with stock, conditions are far more favorable for the trader who wishes to make up his own mind before acting. Almost all of the vital information is available and easy to assess, with profits and losses from individual trades depending largely on the correct interpretation of the data everyone knows.

Although thin margins tend to make the commodity exchanges highly volatile, most commodities trade with daily limits, which helps take some of the wilder gyrations out of daily trading. For instance, if the daily limit in corn is 8¢ and corn closed at $1.15 on the previous day's trading, then, in the current trading day, corn cannot trade above $1.23, or below $1.07.

There is little red tape in commodity trading. Most stock brokerage houses also have a commodity department, or the man who handles your stock transactions may also be able to place your commodity orders. If you are unfamiliar with the details of commodity trading—the size of a contract in various commodities, the required margins, the daily trading limits, etc., most brokerage houses accepting commodity orders will be able to supply you with a brief reference work which explains these details.

Having familiarized yourself with the basic mechanics of commodity trading, you are ready to consider active trading. How much should you commit? Many brokers require a minimum deposit of $1,000 to $2,500 to open a commodity account. Others require only the margin needed for a specific trade.

Orders may be placed with stop-loss protection if you fear that you may miss a turn in a commodity market. But both your decisions to buy and sell and where to place your stops must be based on a trading plan. Without such a plan, you will find yourself engaged in aimless trading.

At first, you may wish to limit your trades to one or two commodities, as you develop a feel for trading. Wheat and soybeans offer good places to begin. But you will want to develop wider knowledge as soon as possible. Occasionally, some commodities will trade flat, offering few opportunities either way. In that case, you will want to have some ideas about a wider range of commodities so that you can find an interesting one in which to trade.

Most traders in commodities rely on both fundamental and technical information in arriving at their trading plan. Fundamentals include such information as an analysis of the demand and supply for specific commodities, crop information, price forecasting, etc. Technical information is derived from the commodity market itself—the pattern of daily trading, attempts to locate trends, the locations of trading ranges, etc. Of course, all of this information has limited usefulness since the object is to predict *future* prices not analyze past trends.

By consulting the following worksheet, you will get some idea of the type of information you will need to develop a trading plan for a commodity.

COMMODITY CONTRACT PURCHASE WORKSHEET

Name of Commodity ______

Position: Long ______ Short* ______ Margin ______
Commission ______

(1) Proposed
Entry Plan: Date ______ Price ______ Quantity ______
Date ______ Price ______ Quantity ______
Date ______ Price ______ Quantity ______

(2) Actual Entry
(if Proposed
Plan is
executed): Date ______ Price ______ Quantity ______
Date ______ Price ______ Quantity ______
Date ______ Price ______ Quantity ______

(3) Liquidation Plan (made at time of Actual Entry):
Final Objective ______ Interim Objective ______
Initial Stop ______ Adjusted Stop ______
Liquidation
Schedule: Date ______ Price ______ Quantity ______
Quantity Remaining ______
Date ______ Price ______ Quantity ______
Quantity Remaining ______
Date ______ Price ______ Quantity ______
Final Date ______

(4) Actual Liquidation (record of actual results using Liquidation Plan):
Reason for Sales: Planned Date ______ Final Date ______
Objective Reached ______
Stop Elected ______

Actual Sales:
Date ______ Quantity ______ Price ______ Net Gain ______
Net Loss ______
Date ______ Quantity ______ Price ______ Net Gain ______
Net Loss ______
Date ______ Quantity ______ Price ______ Net Gain ______
Net Loss ______

(5) Summary: Total Gained ______
Total Lost ______

* Short selling is explained in Chapter 15.

This worksheet could also be expanded to include a summary of the fundamental and technical information that was used in arriving at a given trading plan. It would also be helpful to include an evaluation of your entry plan and liquidation plan in the light of your actual trading experience, if the plan is actually executed. As you trade, you will evolve your own worksheet that best records your decision-making process and the execution of your trading plan.

Commodity trading offers ample opportunities for in-and-out trading in the 1970's. All that is required is that prices fluctuate. However, commodity trading is not for you unless you have both the time and the patience to familiarize yourself with at least the rudiments of trading on these markets. Most brokers can place orders for commodity contracts, but few are in a position to give you expert guidance in trading.

There are two other ways to trade commodities that have attracted some attention recently. One is *options* in commodity futures contracts. This type of trading is young, untested, and not subject, as yet, to adequate regulation; therefore *it is best avoided.* Another method is through *mutual funds* devoted to commodity trading. Some commodity funds were started in the early 1960's, but few were able to turn in a good performance record. Those being started in the 1970's, however, may turn out better and, at least, may be watched for possible commitments once they have proved their effectiveness.

This chapter completes our review of opportunities in the 1970's for investors willing to take some extra chances. In Part V, which follows, we will take a look at some other defensive moves you can take to protect your family from deflation, inflation, and devaluation in the 1970's.

Part V

BACKING UP YOUR INVESTMENTS

CHAPTER 19

Review and Replacements—Time May Be Your Most Important Expenditure

There are some types of investments, like an investment in a home, that an investor can watch every day. But for a great many types of investments, close personal supervision is impossible. Your money is in the bank, but you have no access to the bank's bookkeeping record. Your money is in a stock, but you must rely on the quarterly and annual reports of the company they choose to send you, plus what you can pick up at the annual meeting, if you can spare the time to attend. You may own raw land, but it is 200 miles away, so you are lucky if you see it more than once a year.

There are, of course, individuals who invest with style. When they buy common stock, they buy enough to get elected to the board of directors. When they open a bank account, they deposit an amount sufficiently impressive to make themselves worthy of the attention of the bank officials. When they buy land, they buy enough to be consulted by the town elders before any drastic moves are made concerning land use in the community.

But even if their means permitted, there are many who would not care to be bothered with the petty details of each and every investment they may make. The initial investigations that led to a decision to invest are generally enough to satisfy these individuals, with the day-to-day details of each investment situation of only passing interest.

Most individuals, unwilling or unable to keep a close watch over every single investment in their portfolios, rely on the law of large numbers and averages to protect them. They diversify their portfolios, depending on the very long odds against the possibility that every single one of their investments will turn sour at the same time.

But how much diversification is enough? Gerald Loeb, the noted tape reader and stock market adviser, once gave his answer to diversification: "Put all of your eggs in one basket and watch the basket." He was critical of over-diversification, feeling that an effort to seek safety in large numbers can be overdone by many investors. In the case of stock portfolios, Loeb recommended no more than 10 stocks for the average investor who does not devote full time to the market and his investments. He felt that 10 stocks were about as many as a part-time investor could reasonably expect to follow, review, and decide when to sell. Personal portfolios with 50 or 60 stocks are most probably poorly monitored and supervised by the part-time investor.

Generalizing from Loeb's advice for stock portfolios, it might be said that the proper amount of diversification in a general investment portfolio depends on the amount of time you have to review and evaluate the situations held. There are few things, including even raw land, that you can safely buy and forget. Very often, some of those "forgotten" investments could be earning more for you if they were subjected to a rigorous periodic review and made to prove themselves against new opportunities that have emerged since they were made.

So even though you have filled all of your investment slots with assets—cash in a savings bank, life insurance, a stock portfolio, a no-load mutual fund, raw land, bonds, or whatever appears to have the most promise at the time—your investments planning is far from finished. Each of these assets should be reviewed periodically.

While the concept of a periodic review is fairly well accepted by investors, there is little agreement about the inputs that should go into such a review of holdings. For some, a periodic check to determine whether the brick and mortar behind their paper asset holdings is still in place and functioning is thought sufficient. At the other extreme, there are those who check almost daily on their holdings, with deep brooding (considered to be beneficial) when the daily readings are poor. For most, an occasional period of intense concern, followed by long periods of neglect, is more the pattern.

Seldom is a periodic review of holdings as thorough and vigorous as might be desired, starting from a zero base line and asking what would happen if all of the assets currently being held were sold and replaced by others. One of the reasons zero-base-line reviews are rare is that few investors come to these periodic reviews with a list of candidates, researched and ready for purchase, to replace existing holdings. Ignorance of real alternatives often means that current holdings will remain in place by inertia.

A truly active periodic review of holdings would not only determine whether existing assets are living up to their earlier promise, but it would also evaluate the advantages of replacing any, or all, of these assets with new investments, showing more promise. Most investors fail to take this important second step in their periodic reviews of holdings because they have no real ideas about new investment opportunities that might be available to them at the moment.

Suppose that you have five slots in your current investment portfolio—a savings account, bond holdings, 500 acres of raw land, a stock portfolio, and 200 shares of a no-load mutual fund. An active review of these assets would first, determine whether all of them were still providing the protection and meeting the goals originally set for them; and second, consider alternative investments for each of these five slots, asking the question—"Is there any better way to achieve the protection and performance goals I have set, with investments other than the ones I am holding presently?"

In sum, a periodic review of holdings that does not consider alternative investments is doing only half the job. Zero-base-line portfolio review is preferred—if you sold them all, what would you do now? But even the less drastic "could-I-do-better?" approach will make a periodic review of holdings more meaningful.

In this chapter, we have considered the advantages of changing your portfolio of assets to achieve better yields with less risk. Next we will consider the advantages of changing your base of operations—where you live—to achieve better returns at less risk.

CHAPTER 20

Are There Safer Havens Overseas?

Your home may be your castle, but for many Americans in recent years siege conditions almost seem to prevail. Double locks and safety bars are evidence that many families feel clear and present danger where they live. To date, the violence has been more or less random, but spreading joblessness and the thwarting of the rising expectations many Americans have come to expect in their futures could turn this into a more systematic and threatening situation.

In the last major depression of the 1930's, widespread looting and open revolt never came, somewhat to the surprise of many. Although one-third of the nation was said to be ill-housed, ill-clothed, and ill-fed, this large, deprived minority accepted its fate with an amazing docility. Just why this was so is still largely a mystery to social scientists, but part of the reason may have been the fact that many of these disadvantaged of the 1930's blamed themselves and their own shortcomings for their fate, reflecting the strong popular image of the self-made man at that time.

At the present time, about one-fifth of the total population—20% —is experiencing difficulty in making ends meet. In early 1974, there were just under 5 million unemployed, 11 million on welfare, and almost 25 million living below the economic poverty line, or a total of about 41 million out of the 210 million living in the U.S. While this means that one American in every five probably feels himself economically disadvantaged today, it is still a far cry from the one American in every three who had cause to be dissatisfied in the 1930's. Yet the incidence of random violence, especially in our large urban centers, is far greater than at any time in the 1930's.

That we live today in a violent society is evident. That this violence may increase in the future is a possibility that cannot be ruled out. Many American families have accepted this appraisal of the situation and have given serious consideration to finding safer havens in which to live.

This has led some people to go even further and consider living abroad. While this may be a realistic alternative for the independently wealthy, it is not a practical solution for most, even if they are willing to become expatriates. For most, a decision to live abroad also means a decision to work abroad.

But a decision to live *and* work abroad is not easy to put into effect, nor sometimes easy to live with once it has been accomplished. Even the usually accommodating Swiss, if you request permission to take up residence for longer than three months, will ask you to prove that you have sufficient means to live in Switzerland without engaging in remunerative work. In most countries, you will have to secure work papers if you intend to live and work there. If you have some skill that the country needs, you may be successful. But even then, it is one thing to live abroad on dollars, however devalued; it is quite another to attempt to live on pounds, francs, or lira. Even in Western Europe, living standards are still below those in the United States, and wages and salaries reflect it.

If there are few safe havens overseas where you can live and work, then you may wish to consider possible safe havens overseas for your investments, even though you continue to live in the U.S. We have already discussed the merits of a Swiss bank as a safe haven for your funds (see Chapter 5). Here, we will consider the possibilities of investing abroad.

There are two primary possibilities: (1) you can invest in the common stock of a foreign company, or (2) you can invest in U.S. domiciled companies with important stakes abroad in foreign markets. Either way, you would tend to benefit if economic growth and activity overseas greatly outdistances that within the U.S. in the 1970's.

In the past, it was often said that when the U.S. economy catches a cold, the European economies get pneumonia. Of late, economies of both Western Europe and Japan have developed a momentum of their own, making this appraisal less accurate. However, the U.S. domestic market still remains the largest and most profitable market in the world for most of the economies overseas. And while it may be true that they would no longer collapse if the U.S. economy runs into difficulties, it is also probably true that a depression in the U.S. that lost them this lucrative market would take most of the frosting off their cake. So it appears highly unlikely that investing in foreign companies will be an effective hedge against a depression in the U.S. in the 1970's.

This does not rule out, however, temporary opportunities in the securities of foreign companies during the 1970's. Although national depressions, especially in the U.S. tend to cross international boundaries, there is some unevenness in the rate at which economic difficulties cross borders. Growth spurts in selected foreign countries may, on occasion, be able to overcome the depressing effects of reduced foreign trade, making these nations' companies attractive short-term investments while the international economic weather clears.

If, at any time in the 1970's, you think you see opportunities abroad, you can acquire the common stock of foreign companies by direct investment (some are even listed on U.S. exchanges), or through American Depository Receipts (ADR's). ADR's are stand-ins for foreign securities available to U.S. investors. The U.S. investor buying ADR's pays in dollars for the stock, receives dividends in dollars, and gets dollars when he sells. The amount of cash dividends and the selling price will depend on the operating results of the company in its foreign setting.

Investing abroad was made considerably more attractive for U.S. citizens in early 1974 by the repeal of the interest equalization tax, which had been enacted in 1964, in an effort to curtail the outflow of U.S. dollars. Now, U.S. investors are free to consider foreign securities without any added special tax worries. Following is a reference list of foreign securities actively traded in the U.S., mostly from ADR's. (The world economy is a rapidly changing one in the 1970's; so this list should be viewed as a reference list, not one for unresearched investment.)

Selected Foreign Securities Actively Traded in the U.S.
Unless otherwise indicated, all issues are traded
Over-the-Counter, usually via ADR's.

Argentina	*Australia & New Zealand*
Acindar B	Amalgamated Wireless of Australia
Astra Petroleo	Ampol Exploration
Atanor	Ampol Petroleum
Celulosa Argentina	Australian Consolidated Ind.
Fab. Arg. de Alpargatas	Australian Oil & Gas
General Fabril. Fin.	Broken Hill
Ika-Renault	Coles (G. J.) & Co.
Magnasco y Cia	Custom Credit Corp.
Molinos Rio de la Plata	Interstate Oil
Ernesto Torquist	Lake View & Star
	Mount Isa Mines

Selected Foreign Securities Actively Traded in the U.S. (cont.)

Myers Emporium
New Zealand Petroleum
Phillip Morris of Australia
Santos
Union Carbide of Australia

Belgium

Ford of Belgium
Petrofina
Photo Gavaert ADR
Union Miniere De Haut Katanga

France

Financier de Suez
Librairie Hachette
Machines Bull
Michelin
Pechiney
St. Gobain
Source Perrier

Germany

AEG-Telefunken
Allianz Insurance
Badische Anilin & Soda
Commerzbank
Daimler-Benz
Deutsche Bank
Dresdner Bank
Farbenfabriken Bayer
Farbwerke Hoechst
Karstadt Inc.
Lufthansa
Rhine Westphalia Elect.
Schering A. G.
Siemens A. G.
Volkeswagenwerk

Great Britain, Republic of South Africa & Rhodesia

American S. Africa In. (NYS)
Anglo-Amer. Corp. S.A.
Anglo-Equadorian Oilfields
Assoc. British Foods
Beecham Group
Blyvooruitzicht Gold Min.
Bowater Paper
British-Amer. Tobacco (ASE)
British Leyland
British Oxygen
British Petroleum (ASE)
BSR
Buffelsfontein
Burma Mines
Burmah Oil
Carreras
Charter Consol.
Consol. Gold Fields
Daggafontein Min.
De Beers Cons. Min.
Doornfontein
Durban Roodepoort
East Daggafontein Min.
East Rand Prop. Min.
Elsburg Gold Min.
Free State Geduld Minl
Gestetner
Glaxo
Great Universal Stores
Harteebeestfontein Gold Min.
Harmony Gold Min.

Great Britian, Republic of South Africa & Rhodesia (cont.)

International Computers
International Distiliers
Kloof
Lorraine Gold Min.
Middle-Witwaters
Nchanga Consol. Copper
Orange Free State Inv. Tr.
Ozalid Co.
Palabora Min.
Penguin Books
Potgietersrust Plat.
Premier Consol. Oilfields
Pres. Brand Gold Min.
Pres. Steyn Gold Min.
Rank Organisation "A"
Rhokana Corp.
Rio Tinto Zinc
St. Helena Gold Min.
St. John Del Rey Min.
Shell Transport (NYS)
Stilfontein Gold Min.
Tanganyika Concess. Ltd.
Tesco Stores

Selected Foreign Securities Actively Traded in the U.S. (cont.)

Toreodor Royalty
Trinidad Petroleum
Tube Investments
Ultra Electric
Ultramar
Unilever (NYS)
Union Corp.
Vaal Reef
Venterspost Gold Min.
Virginia O.F.S. Gold Min.
Welkom Gold Min.
West Driefontein
Western Areas
Western Deep Level
Western Holdings
West Rand Inv. Tr.
Western Stockholders Inv.
Winkelhaak Min.
Zambian Anglo-Amer. Ord.
Zandpan Gold Min.

Holland

L. Van Der Grinten
Heineken's Bierbrouweij
Kon. Ned Hoogovens
Kon. Zout-Organon
Nationale Nederlanden
Ned. Ford Automobiel
J. V. Magazin "De Bijenkorf"
Philips Gloeilampen
Royal Dutch New York Shares
Unilever N.V. New York Shares

Honduras

Banco Atlantida
Tabacalera Hond.

Israel

Amer.-Israel Paper Mills (ASE)
Ampal-Amer.
Bank Leumi
Israel Devel. Corp.
Israel Discount Bank
PEC Israel Ec. Corp.

Italy

Fiat
Montecatini-Edison
Olivetti
Pirelli
La Rinascente
Snia Viscosa

Japan

Canon Camera
Chugai Pharm.
Fuji Photo
Hitachi
Honda Motors
Japan Airlines
Kansai Elec.
Nippon Elec.
Nissan Motors
Shin Mitsubishi
Sony
Tokio Marine & Fire Ins.
Toshiba
Toyota Motors

Mexico

Altos Hornos de Mexico
Banco Nacional
Celanese Mexicana
Cigarrera La Moderna
Fabricas Auto-Max
Firme
Fundidora de Monterrey
Nacional Financiera
Telefonos de Mexico

Peru

Backus & Johnson's Brewery
Empress Elect. Ass.
Energ. Hidr. Andina.
Tejidos La Union

Philippines

Bogo Medellin
Hawaiian Philippine
LePanto Consol. Mining
Marinduque Mng. & Ind.
Philex Mining
San Miguel Corp.

Selected Foreign Securities Actively Traded in the U.S. (cont.)

Sweden	*Switzerland*
Alfa-Laval	F. Hoffmann-LaRoche
Electrolux	Nestle-Alimentana
Ericsson	Swiss Bank
Swedish Ball Bearing	Swiss Credit Bk.
Swedish Match 'B'	Union Bank of Switzerland

ASE—American Stock Exchange
NYS—New York Stock Exchange
TOR—Toronto Stock Exchange

You may notice that there are no Canadian companies on this list. The economies of the U.S. and Canada have become so closely intermeshed in recent years that it seems extremely unlikely that the Canadian economy could buck any serious setback in the domestic U.S. economy, even for short periods of time. Therefore, as a rule in the 1970's, when you would not buy U.S. stocks, you should not consider Canadian stocks either.

Another possible approach to taking temporary positions that might benefit from continued economic health abroad while the U.S. economy is experiencing heavy-going is through U.S. companies doing a sizable percentage of their total business abroad. If a high percentage of their sales is dependent on developments on foreign markets, these companies might do better during domestic setbacks than U.S. companies doing most of their business exclusively on domestic markets. Following is a selected list of U.S. domiciled companies doing a significant share of their total business abroad, and is provided as a reference checklist.

Selected U.S. Companies Making a Significant Share of Their Total Sales Abroad

COMPANY	FOREIGN SALES AS PERCENTAGE OF TOTAL SALES	WHERE FOREIGN SALES ARE MADE
American Smelting & Refining	65%	Australia, Peru, Mexico
Schlumberger	59	France, Canada
Colgate-Palmolive	55	Worldwide
Caterpillar Tractor	53	Worldwide
CPC International	50	Worldwide
Otis Elevator	50	Worldwide
Exxon Corp.	50	Worldwide
Pfizer	47	Britain, Europe, Latin America
Occidental Petroleum	46	Middle East, So. Amer., Africa
USM	46	Britain, Europe, So. Am.
Gulf Oil	45	Middle East, So. Amer., Canada
Mobil Oil	45	Canada, Middle East
National Cash Register	45	Worldwide

Selected U.S. Companies Making a Significant Share of Their Total Sales Abroad (cont.)

COMPANY	FOREIGN SALES AS PERCENTAGE OF TOTAL SALES	WHERE FOREIGN SALES ARE MADE
Standard Oil of California	45	Middle East, Indonesia, So. Amer.
H. J. Heinz	44	Worldwide
Chesebrough-Pond's	43	Eur., Can., Latin Amer.
Gillette	43	Worldwide
Black & Decker	42	Export Sales
International Tel. & Tel.	42	Can., Eur., Latin Am.
Dow Chemical	40	Worldwide
Englehard Minerals & Chem.	40	Britain, Europe, Japan
Texaco	40	Worldwide
International Business Machines	39	Worldwide
Singer	37	Eur., Latin Amer.
American Standard	36	Europe
Minnesota Mining & Mfg.	36	Europe, Canada, Australia
Warner Lambert	36	Worldwide
First National City Corp.	35	Worldwide
Honeywell	35	Eur., British Commonwealth
F. W. Woolworth	35	Can., Germany, Britain
Sperry Rand	34	Europe, Japan
W. R. Grace	33	Latin America
Coca-Cola	31	Worldwide
Eastman Kodak	31	Worldwide
Xerox	30	Europe, Japan
Firestone Tire & Rubber	29	Worldwide
Union Carbide	29	Worldwide
Uniroyal	27	Canada, Mexico
Ford Motor	26	Germany, Brit., Aust.
International Harvester	25	Can., Eur., Africa
Proctor & Gamble	25	Britain, Eur., Lat. Am.
Chrysler	24	Worldwide
Monsanto	24	Can., Latin Am., Eur.
General Foods	21	Canada
General Motors	19	Germany, Britain, Australia
E. I. DuPont	18	Export Sales, Europe
Litton Industries	17	Europe, Latin Amer.
General Electric	16	So. Amer., Canada, Italy
Swift	16	Canada, Britain, Germany

In this chapter, we have considered going far afield in search of safe yields in the 1970's. In Chapter 21, we will consider staying close to home and owning your own business as a means for seeking safer yields in the 1970's.

CHAPTER 21

Putting You and Your Money in One Basket—Owning Your Own Business

Self-employment has its rewards, but the risks are high. Many of the self-employed in the United States work for themselves only part of the time, holding on to a regular job that takes most of their working day. About one-third of those with second jobs—moonlighters—are self-employed on a part-time basis.

Self-employment covers a multitude of pursuits, including such things as poodle breeding, farming, running a business out of the home, "mom-and-pop" retail shops, and respectable-sized family manufacturing concerns. Every day about 1,000 businesses are formed in the U.S., some of them part-time businesses, but an estimated 930 firms also close each day. Still, about one family in ten operates some kind of business.

But the most important question for you to answer is: Should I start a business of my own? The overwhelming majority of new business firms fail, most of them in the first two years of operation. So you will have to examine your reasons and qualifications very carefully before deciding to go into business for yourself. Wanting to be your own boss, while an appealing reason, is not one of the primary requirements for successful business entry. Below is a brief summary of the questions the U.S. Government's Small Business Administration feels that you should be able to answer before attempting to start a business.

- Are you the right type to start a business—do you have leadership traits, organizing ability, perseverance, and enough physical energy?
- Can you really succeed? What talents and skills do you bring to the business; have you correctly estimated sales and operating expenses; what kind of profit can you make (and will this amount be satisfactory to you)?
- Do you know enough about pricing your product, servicing, keeping business records, tax problems, and the physical plant required to house your business to keep it operating smoothly?
- Finally, and perhaps most importantly, have you made a correct estimate of your capital needs, including enough funds to tide you over in the early months until revenues from sales can finally begin to reduce the start-up expenses?

There are other questions on the SBA's checklist, but these should keep you busy for a while if you are considering starting a new business.

One person it will probably pay to consult is your local banker, even if you do not think you need any extra start-up capital to get your new enterprise rolling. A local banker usually reviews a large number of business proposals each year and often has a feel about the chance of success. If he likes your business plan, you should have more confidence in it. If he sees flaws, you should pay close attention—he may know what he is talking about.

Suppose you need the banker's help? Then he will have to like your business plan. If you have no track record in running a business, he may still lend you the money, but it will be your own personal credit rating, rather than the business and its prospects, that will probably impress him the most in making the loan. For a discussion of ways to establish a credit rating at a bank see Chapter 6.

What if the amount you can get at the bank is not enough? Of course, there are your personal savings. In fact, the banker may be willing to give you more if he knows you are kicking in a big chunk of your own hard-earned savings. There are friends and relatives (see Chapter 6 for a discussion of problems connected with borrowing from this source). In some lines you may find that you can get trade credit from suppliers that will provide you with inventory for between 30 and 90 days, if the initial orders are small, even without an established business credit rating. However, this just about exhausts your sources of financing if you have only a business plan on paper.

Of course, you may have what some call a "concept" business proposal.

When you are selling a concept—a new product, a new process, a new marketing idea, you will be looking for venture capital. Where can you find venture capital? Again, a good place to start is your local banker. He may know of some wealthy individual or individuals that you might approach. There are venture capital companies, some national in scope and large enough to be listed on the NYSE, that make their money by locating and assisting promising new business ventures. Some of these companies are regional and local. Your banker should be able to supply you with a list of the venture capital companies that are active in your part of the country. There are also the Small Business Investment Companies (SBIC's) that operate as lenders of last resort in financing your business. If your idea or concept has real merit, you will most likely be able to find some backing among wealthy individuals or local venture capital groups. Do not be discouraged by a turndown. Turndowns are common, but there is little evidence that a good business idea ever failed to find backing, even in the most unpromising times.

Assuming your business is a success, you may have difficulties getting your money out of the business when you want to retire. In an earlier time, fathers typically passed their businesses on to their sons. But this is out of style in the present age, with few sons showing much interest in following in their fathers' footsteps. Of course, this could change in the 1970's, especially if the opportunities available for new college graduates continue to narrow as they have in the last few years.

Another way out in the 1960's was to go public, sell stock, and then tempt one of the accumulating conglomerates with the owner's controlling block of stock. This exit may be less feasible in the 1970's for two reasons: (1) the public may be less enthusiastic about new common stock issues in companies going public for the first time and (2) conglomerates may be more interested in divesting themselves of their past mistakes than gobbling up new companies. So you may be less anxious to spend 18 hours a day running your own business if you feel that there is little chance of getting something back for this extra effort when it comes time to consider retiring.

There is another on-going consideration connected with owning your own business at the present time, namely, the matter of fringe benefits. When you are your own boss, you will have to pay for your own fringes—life insurance, health insurance, pension plans, sick leave plans, even pay your own Social Security. This is a very important consideration in our present day economy when family welfare programs have become "institutionalized" and built into the compensation system, with the fringes bulking larger every year in the total compensation given employees. And many of these costs are cheaper when provided under the large group contract plans that likely will not be available to your small business firm.

All of this may help explain why many of the self-employed choose to run their own business ventures after hours from a full-time job. Also, 9-to-5 may look good compared with the 7:30 A.M. to 9:15 P.M. worked by many people who are their own bosses. Financial factors, our primary concern here, may not be the most important considerations in deciding whether to own your own business.

In this chapter, we have considered the financial aspects of the most self-reliant type of investing you can undertake—owning your own business. In the next chapter, we will discuss the prospects of remaining self-reliant even though your financial planning runs into difficulties.

CHAPTER 22

How to Bail Out if Everything Goes Against You

You do not have to recall Robert Burns's mice and men to know that plans often go awry. Money may flow in, but it also flows out.

But there are degrees of trouble. If your debts are numerous and many are overdue, you may think you have troubles. But if you are borrowing money to make payments on money you borrowed earlier, you are in condition red. And when the sources of these secondary borrowings shut their loan windows to you, then you are in real trouble.

What should you do when you are deep in wall-to-wall financial trouble? You might simply walk out; some do. However, not only does this solution lack style; but, more seriously, it also does irreparable damage to your ability to make a financial comeback, in almost any place and at any time in the future.

At a time of trouble, it might occur to you to consider the offers of the personal finance companies to help you consolidate your debts. In most cases, you should politely but firmly decline such offers of help. For one thing, most of your overdue bills are probably already costing you interest; so if you now borrow from the finance company, you will be paying interest on top of interest. Furthermore, even if the finance company is willing to lend you enough to extinguish your existing debts completely, you will often be paying higher interest payments to the finance company than you are now paying your creditors. For instance, on an overdue department store bill or a gasoline credit card bill you will be paying 18% at an annual rate. If you pay off these bills with money the finance company lends you, most likely you will be paying the small loan company 24–36% at an annual rate (see Chapter 6). It is difficult to see how you can benefit by paying off an 18% loan with money that costs you 24% or more.

Admittedly, a single monthly payment might be more convenient than a number of smaller payments each month. If this aspect of consolidation attracts you, you might try the bank. A bank is sometimes willing to consider a consolidation loan. If you can get a bank loan at a lower rate of annual interest, say 12%, you might consider extinguishing some of your more pressing bills if the effective rate you are paying currently on these overdue bills is above the rate the banks charge you.

What if the small loan company's rates look too steep and the bank turns you down? You might try appealing to your creditors. Repossessing a dining-room table and chairs is an unpleasant and often unprofitable business, so most creditors will at least be willing to listen to any reasonable plan to pay off the debt, even at a reduced monthly rate.

In some cases, your creditor may even refer you to a debt counselor. However, make certain that the debt counselor you consult has community support; preferably, he should be part of a nonprofit counseling agency. (There are unscrupulous debt counselors.) But a reliable debt counselor can be of great service, acting as a buffer between you and your creditors and assisting you in rearranging the large debt repayments "due next week" into more manageable monthly installments. If, even with the help of a debt counselor, you fail to satisfy your creditors, the next step is personal bankruptcy. This type of solution to family financial problems has been growing in recent years, with over 90% of all bankruptcies in the United States being the family-type rather than commercial bankruptcy.

There are two avenues open in bankruptcy, a Chapter XIII bankruptcy, or a straight bankruptcy. Under a Chapter XIII bankruptcy (so-called because it is based on Chapter XIII of the Federal Bankruptcy Law), much the same happens as would be the case if you went to a debt counselor, but here the debt pooling is not voluntary. Under the supervision of a judge of one of the Federal district courts, the debtor, the creditors, and a referee get together and work out a way for the debtor to settle with his creditors in a series of regular installments.

Or you may petition for voluntary bankruptcy the regular way. In this case you must submit a complete listing of all assets and liabilities together with a $50 filing fee. After this is done, the rest is fairly routine. Except for clothing, tools, some household goods and in some states, a homestead, all of the other assets you own are liquidated and the proceeds distributed among the creditors. This wipes the slate clean of everything except the bankruptcy record itself which will continue to hang over the debtor for the rest of his life.

There is a last step beyond voluntary bankruptcy—you might wait for your creditors to bring bankruptcy proceedings against you. But there is very little difference in the long run.

Although it might sound a bit trivial, it should be pointed out that, regardless of how you choose to go bankrupt, there are likely to be legal fees on top of everything else, not to mention the $50 filing fee in the case of voluntary bankruptcy. Any way you look at it, bankruptcy of any type has few features to recommend it. And although more and more individuals have been turning to personal bankruptcy to get out from under their debts in recent years, it is not likely to become the preferred method for solving family financial problems in the 1970's.

Clearly, the best defense against personal bankruptcy is sound family financial planning. If you are currently borrowing money to meet the payments on money you borrowed yesterday, there may still be time to mend your family finances. Re-read Chapter 1, study the summary which follows, and get ready to face the 1970's.

CONCLUSION: TEN RULES FOR FINANCIAL WELL-BEING IN TODAY'S ECONOMY

Conclusion

Ten Rules That Will Give You the Self-Reliance and Flexibility to Weather—and Profit from—Inflation, Deflation, and Devaluation in the 1970's

Rule 1:

Set aside ("free-up") 10% of your before-tax income on the receipt of each paycheck—and test higher set-asides in steps: 11%, 12%, 13%, etc.—until you find the level of funds you can safely free and yet maintain your family's living standards.

IMPLEMENTATION:

Put these freed funds in a savings account until they can be utilized. Use them in this order: First, to implement Rule 2 and Rule 3; then, to implement Rules 4 through 8.

REASONING BEHIND THE RULE:

This 10% rule for freeing funds (and the further step-ups recommended) permit you to establish budget controls without all of the fuss of taking $11.73 from one account to make up a deficit in another in your family budget.

WHERE TO LOOK FOR A FULLER DISCUSSION OF RULE 1:

The 10% Rule: Chapter 8
Where to look for more funds that might be freed: Chapters 2, 3, 4, and 7
Where to put your freed funds for safekeeping: Chapters 5 and 9
Ways to supplement your present funds through borrowing: Chapter 6

Rule 2:

Accumulate savings equal to 6 months of before-tax income.

IMPLEMENTATION:

Put these funds in a savings account, U.S. government bonds (Series E or H), or high-grade corporate bonds.

REASONING BEHIND THE RULE:

These are your emergency funds; so you want them highly liquid. In addition, they might as well be earning you some return.

WHERE TO LOOK FOR A FULLER DISCUSSION OF RULE 2:

Introduction, Chapter 1, and especially Chapter 8.

For Implementation: Chapter 9

Rule 3:

Provide life insurance protection equal to 5 years of your average estimated annual before-tax wages and salaries.

IMPLEMENTATION:

A mix of ordinary, term, and group, if the group is not job-connected.

REASONING BEHIND THE RULE:

This is your family's defense and the nucleus of your estate.

WHERE TO LOOK FOR A FULLER DISCUSSION OF RULE 3:

Chapter 4

Rule 4:

For additional *current* income buy high-quality bonds.

IMPLEMENTATION:

Limit your buying to U.S. government, municipal, and corporates rated A or better. Especially attractive if available at 8%, or better, yields. Check call features on corporates.

REASONING BEHIND THE RULE:

Bonds nail down high yields when they are available. This is for those who need more income *now.* If you can afford to wait, you will find more attractive *long-term* yields under Rules 5 through 7.

WHERE TO LOOK FOR A FULLER DISCUSSION OF RULE 4:

Chapter 9

Rule 5:

For Income Plus, use dollar cost averaging to accumulate (1) no-load mutual funds with *income-appreciation* as objective and (2) common stocks with proven, stable income and earnings patterns.

IMPLEMENTATION:

If you feel that you have little time to supervise your portfolio, stick to no-load mutual funds in meeting this objective.

REASONING BEHIND THE RULE:

The use of dollar cost averaging permits you to ignore the problem of timing your purchases. No-load mutual funds would free you from the burdens of stock portfolio supervision. When you do buy common stocks, sticking to reliable cash dividend payers, which sell products that need constant replacement or which have had proven growth in the past, will ease your problems of stock selection.

WHERE TO LOOK FOR A FULLER DISCUSSION OF RULE 5:

Chapter 14, especially.

For dollar cost averaging: Chapter 12.

No-load funds: Chapter 17

Rule 6:

For Appreciation Plus, use dollar cost averaging to accumulate (1) no-load mutual funds with *appreciation* as objective and (2) common stocks with historical growth records and potential for the 1970's.

IMPLEMENTATION:

Stick to no-load funds if you feel you do not have the time to search out stocks with good appreciation potentials for the 1970's.

REASONING BEHIND THE RULE:

For comments on dollar cost averaging and no-load funds, see this section under Rule 5, above. The selection analysis required for buying common stocks limits it to those with time and the inclination.

WHERE TO LOOK FOR A FULLER DISCUSSION OF RULE 6:

Chapter 14

For dollar cost averaging: Chapter 12

No-load funds: Chapter 17

Rule 7:

Without specialized knowledge, limit your purchase of real assets to mint stamps and coins. In all cases, defer real estate purchases until the second half of the decade of the 1970's.

IMPLEMENTATION:

Place your orders in advance of issue with mints and postal authorities.

REASONING BEHIND THE RULE:

Mint stamps and coins require no special talents to evaluate and you are certain to get what you pay for. The same cannot be said of any other real asset. The most attractive real estate investments are office buildings and commercial property, and they are currently going vacant, so avoid until the last half of the 1970's.

WHERE TO LOOK FOR A FULLER DISCUSSION OF RULE 7:

Raw land: Chapter 10
Stamps, coins, gemstones, antiques, art objects, etc.: Chapter 11
Real estate: Chapter 13
Your own business: Chapter 21

Rule 8:

For in-and-out trading in the 1970's, use puts and calls for going short and long on common stocks. Consider commodity trading for added short-term profits.

IMPLEMENTATION:

You will have to be willing to do your homework if you are going to trade either stocks or commodities. Not for the timid and not for the lazy.

REASONING BEHIND THE RULE:

There is one thing certain about both common stocks and commodity contracts—they always fluctuate. You have to be alert to catch the swings, but there are short-turn profits to be made if you are willing to devote the time and patience you will need to select and time your buys and sells. For short-term periods only in the 1970's, you also might consider foreign stocks when the outlook overseas is brighter than at home. Over the long haul, we live in a global economy, with few places to hide.

WHERE TO LOOK FOR A FULLER DISCUSSION OF RULE 8:

Puts and calls: Chapter 16
For an introduction to short selling: Chapter 15
Commodity trading: Chapter 18
Foreign stocks: Chapter 20

Rule 9:

Diversify your investment holdings, but do not take on more situations than you can supervise in the time you have available for investment decision-making.

IMPLEMENTATION:

Try to limit yourself to 10 different investment situations, if each requires a completely new analytical framework to reach a decision. In any event, do not buy into more situations than you can conveniently watch. This may be one instance where your stomach is bigger than your eyes.

REASONING BEHIND THE RULE:

The 1970's will be a time of transition. Great and often disturbing changes will take place in the economy. Markets for stocks and all types of investments will be nervous. All of your investments will require careful watching in the 1970's. One way you can make certain that you have the time to follow developments closely is to limit the number of situations you need to be knowledgeable about.

WHERE TO LOOK FOR A FULLER DISCUSSION OF RULE 9:

Chapter 19

Rule 10:

Learn to be a self-reliant investor in the 1970's. Keep alert and stay flexible.

IMPLEMENTATION:

The only way you can be self-reliant in managing your investments is to understand fully the reasons for each and every buy and sell order you place. This will keep you alert, and it will provide you with the knowledge that will enable you to be flexible—that is, both able and willing to move in and out of situations on short notice.

REASONING BEHIND THE RULE:

It is always wise to know what you are doing. But this may be essential in the 1970's. There may be little margin for error in investment planning in these years. Hard decisions will have to be made by everyone—businesses, governments, and families. Vast changes in values and practices must take place in almost every sector of society. In the economy, these changes seem to assure a shakedown in almost every industrial sector. If these shakedowns come a sector at a time, we will say that each is experiencing its own depression, as aerospace has been experiencing over the last few years. But if these sector shakedowns bunch, we will most certainly call the results a national economic depression. So your investment planning in the 1970's must be flexible enough to allow, at a minimum, for a "rolling" depression that strikes one sector of the economy after another, as each adjusts to the requirements of the world in the 1970's. At a maximum, your personal investment planning must be able to stand up during an economy-wide depression, if these needed adjustments of values and processes happen in a large number of industrial sectors at the same time.

WHERE TO LOOK FOR A FULLER DISCUSSION OF RULE 10:

For the reasons you need to be self-reliant and flexible in the 1970's: Introduction

How to keep your head in times of extreme adversity: Chapter 22

How to be self-reliant and flexible in the 1970's: Chapters 1–21

GOOD LUCK!

Index